◆ © MARK WILSON

© BRUCE YUAN-YUE BI

URBAN
TAPESTRY
SERIES
TOWERY
PUBLISHING, INC.

TORONTO

TORONTO:
The World within a City

INTRODUCTION BY:
Edwin Mirvish and
David Mirvish

ART DIRECTION BY:
Robert Shatzer

▲ © STEVE EPRILE / HOT SHOTS STOCK SHOTS, INC.

TORONTO:
The World within a City

Contents

◆ ©JAN BUTCHOFSKY-HOUSER / HOUSERSTOCK, INC.

By Edwin and David Mirvish

EDWIN MIRVISH: When I
moved to Toronto almost 80 years ago, I thought that it was a dull city. I was only nine years old, but compared to my former home—Washington, D.C.—Toronto just didn't seem to have the same excitement.

The population then was about 500,000, and although Toronto seemed like a nice place, it lacked the big-city hustle and bustle of Washington. It seemed to me to be nothing but a collection of homes and churches. There were the blue laws—everything was closed on Sundays, and you couldn't even buy a newspaper or a bottle of milk. Needless to say, there was no entertainment allowed on Sundays as well.

How things have changed. The past three-quarters of a century has seen Toronto grow into one of the most exciting places in the world.

Today, the population of Greater Toronto is 2.5 million. It's a place that can satisfy the tastes of everyone, from those who are looking for a nice city (of homes and churches!) to an exciting, world-class, big city of entertainment, business, and commerce.

We are now the third-most-important theatre city in the world, behind only New York and London. There are more than 200 professional theatre and dance organizations that form the Toronto Theatre Alliance, representing everything from large theatres to small venues to dinner theatres. ▶

◆ © FRANCO ROSSI

DAVID MIRVISH:

As owner and producer for two theatres in Toronto—the Royal Alexandra Theatre and the Princess of Wales Theatre—and operator of the Canon Theatre, formerly known as the Pantages Theatre, I have had the privilege and opportunity to travel all over the world in the search for entertainment. I have never lost my enthusiasm for visiting other cities. Being naturally competitive, I always compare these cities with Toronto. Invariably, I come home stimulated, but also grateful for what is one of Toronto's finest qualities: it is an eminently livable city.

The 1960s were a turning point in Toronto's history. It decided that it was a city of neighbourhoods, that people were more important than cars, that we would not build an expressway through the centre of downtown. Toronto decided that housing in the centre of the city was important. Toronto decided that the Annex, Rosedale, West College Street, Cabbagetown, and Yorkville were all ideal neighbourhoods for living, shopping, and eating.

At the first part of the 1960s, Toronto embraced growth and the new at the expense of its older buildings. Built in 1961, the O'Keefe Centre—now named the Hummingbird Centre for the Performing Arts—with its 3,200 seats, was the new kid in town. The Royal Alexandra Theatre, with 1,500 seats, built in 1907, was scheduled for demolition. However, my father, who loved the old building and its ornate plaster ornamentation, rescued it from becoming a parking lot. He said that he would preserve it for at least five years as a live theatre. That was in 1963. Now, all these years later, the Royal Alexandra Theatre is approaching its

From left: David and Edwin Mirvish

© BORIS SPREMO, C.M.

100th birthday, and it's thriving. As is the Princess of Wales Theatre, which is also owned by my family. Built in 1993, the theater has seating for 2,000. Since opening, the Princess of Wales Theatre has been home to some of the greatest shows of our time including *Miss Saigon*, *Les Miserables*, and Disney's *The Lion King*.

EDWIN: The Royal Alexandra and Princess of Wales theatres draw audiences from all parts of Canada and the United States. They are major tourist attractions. We're proud to have been able to offer them as just a part of what makes Toronto such a lively, engaging place to live or to visit.

There are many other features that make this such an interesting and yet comfortable place. You can enjoy fine food from every part of the world. Toronto is a city of parks and greenery, with Riverdale and High parks being two of the largest. It's a place where big business and commerce thrive, and yet it's a place where you can live in quiet residential areas. It's got a full slate of exciting major sports. And, the arts are always first-rate, from live theatre and other performing arts to visual arts and architecture.

Toronto has a very fine zoo with a train that runs through the park and allows the passengers to see many of the animals roaming wild.

Toronto is an educational centre, and is home to the University of Toronto, York University, and Ryerson University. The University of Toronto alone has more than 52,000 students. In addition, the Toronto Conservatory

© JONATHAN POSTAL / TOWERY PUBLISHING, INC.

© JONATHAN POSTAL / TOWERY PUBLISHING, INC.

Art Gallery of Toronto Director Matthew Teitelbaum

of Music has trained musicians known throughout Canada and the world.

Another big change from when I moved here is that Toronto has become truly multicultural. It has a mosaic representing hundreds of different countries and dozens of different cultures. These people settle in Toronto and find here the opportunity to express themselves in their own individual and creative way. This mix of nationalities with each one bringing its own culture makes Toronto the interesting, attractive, and exciting city that it is.

DAVID: Yes, Toronto has become a home for people from all over the world. If you visit Jarvis Collegiate, a downtown high school, you will meet many students for whom English is a second language. In fact, 69 different languages are represented in the school. Our welcoming attitudes toward people from cultures throughout the world have helped make this a diverse community. This hasn't always been so, but it is today.

© BRAD CROOKS

By the same token, our attitudes about the past have also changed dramatically. Several decades ago, "progress" meant tearing down anything old and replacing it as fast as possible. Today, Toronto cherishes its past and would never allow a great building to be torn down. At the same time, we enthusiastically embrace the present and the future, as evidenced by the outstanding modern architecture that stands out in the city.

One of the most appealing aspects of life here is, of course, the vibrant arts community. The five major arts

© JONATHAN POSTAL / TOWERY PUBLISHING, INC.

Foreground: Ballet Creole Director Patrick Parson

organizations have extraordinary leadership, and have all moved to a position of international prominence as a result.

William Thorsell—recently appointed the president of the Royal Ontario Museum, one of the largest museums in North America—is about to embark on a seven-year plan that will give a complete renewal and result in an enormous expansion to the present plant.

Matthew Teitelbaum, the director at the Art Gallery of Ontario, has both grown the permanent collection and made the museum more appealing to the public through the programming of exhibitions, lectures, research, education, and travel.

The National Ballet of Canada, under the leadership of Artistic Director James Kudelka, has recently enjoyed such great artistic and financial triumphs as *The Firebird*, while also continuing its program of new ballets, as well as a consolidation of its facilities in the recently built Walter Carsen Centre.

Edward Smith has recently become executive director of the Toronto Symphony Orchestra after spending 18 years with Sir Simon Rattle at the City of Birmingham Symphony Orchestra. Roy Thomson Hall, the orchestra's home, will complete a $20 million acoustical refit by Russell Johnson by mid-2002.

And, Richard Bradshaw, General Director of the Canadian Opera Company, has breathed creative life at the highest level into the company's artistic achievement, and has grown his audience considerably.

Toronto is also the home of more than 200 professional theatre and dance companies that are members of the Toronto Theatre Alliance, an organization with which my

© JONATHAN POSTAL / TOWERY PUBLISHING, INC.

From left: Sandy Jobin-Bevans and Doug Morency of The Second City

© BETSY MOLNAR

father and I are proud to be actively affiliated. Each month, there are some 75 productions being staged, reaching some 7 million people a year, about half of whom are visitors to Toronto. I always look at the newspapers (we are blessed with four major papers here) to see what is playing at the 70 theatre venues in Toronto—places like Centre Stage, Tarragon Theatre, Theatre Passe Muraille, Factory Theatre, du Maurier Theatre, Premiere Dance Theatre, Buddies in Bad Times Theatre, Toronto Dance Theatre, and Second City. Our larger venues include Roy Thomson Hall, Massey Hall, Hummingbird Centre for the Performing Arts, Pantages Theatre, Elgin Theatre, Wintergarden Theatre, and Toronto Performing Arts Centre. The offerings are varied and exciting, spanning the gamut of live theatre.

© FRANCO ROSSI

We also must mention a few important specialty museums. The Ydessa Hendeles Art Foundation and the Power Plant both curate extraordinarily fine contemporary exhibitions. Likewise, the Gardiner Museum of Ceramic Art, Museum for Textiles, the Bata Shoe Museum, and University of Toronto Art Centre all hold exceptional exhibitions.

And, rounding out Toronto's cultural calendar is a full slate of festivals. The Toronto International Film Festival, directed by Piers Handling each September, attracts audiences and creative talent in overwhelming numbers. After more than 25 years, it is thought to be one of the two most important film festivals in the world. (Perhaps in part because of this fine festival, in the summer of 2000 more than 70 films were produced in Toronto, a city which seems to be rivalling Hollywood in terms of cinematic productions.) ▶

▲ © BRANDON KLAYMAN

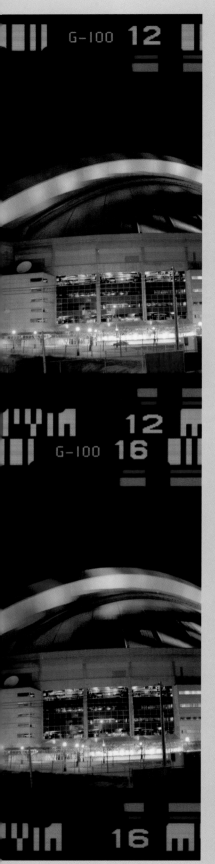

Every other year there is a great World Stage, Toronto's International Theatre Festival, organized by Don Shipley. He recently brought us both Peter Brook and Ariane Mnouchkine, two giants of European theatre.

Each fall, the Royal Agricultural Winter Fair presents a view of rural Ontario and a great horse show. It has been a tradition in my family for some years now to try to buy some of the prize-winning maple syrup.

The International Festival of Authors, created and directed by Greg Gatenby, is approaching its 20th season. This festival has been hailed as the largest literary event in the world; in 2000, it attracted some 60 renowned novel-

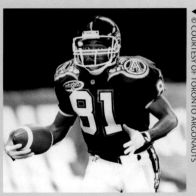

ists, poets, biographers, and playwrights from 20 countries. It also features many popular special events; at the 2000 festival, J.K. Rowling—beloved creator of the Harry Potter phenomenon—gave a rare North American reading before 30,000 people at the SkyDome.

Oh, yes, the SkyDome! There's tremendous support for the pro teams that play here, such as the Blue Jays, two-time winners of the World Series. The SkyDome is also home to

the Toronto Argonauts football team, and is the site for major events and shows of all sorts.

The new Air Canada Centre houses our hockey and basketball teams, the Toronto Maple Leafs and the Toronto Raptors, and regularly sells out 20,000 seats to concert attractions.

EDWIN: Other "sports"—or perhaps "art forms"—that Toronto residents and visitors are avid fans of are shopping and dining. As mentioned, there's wonderful

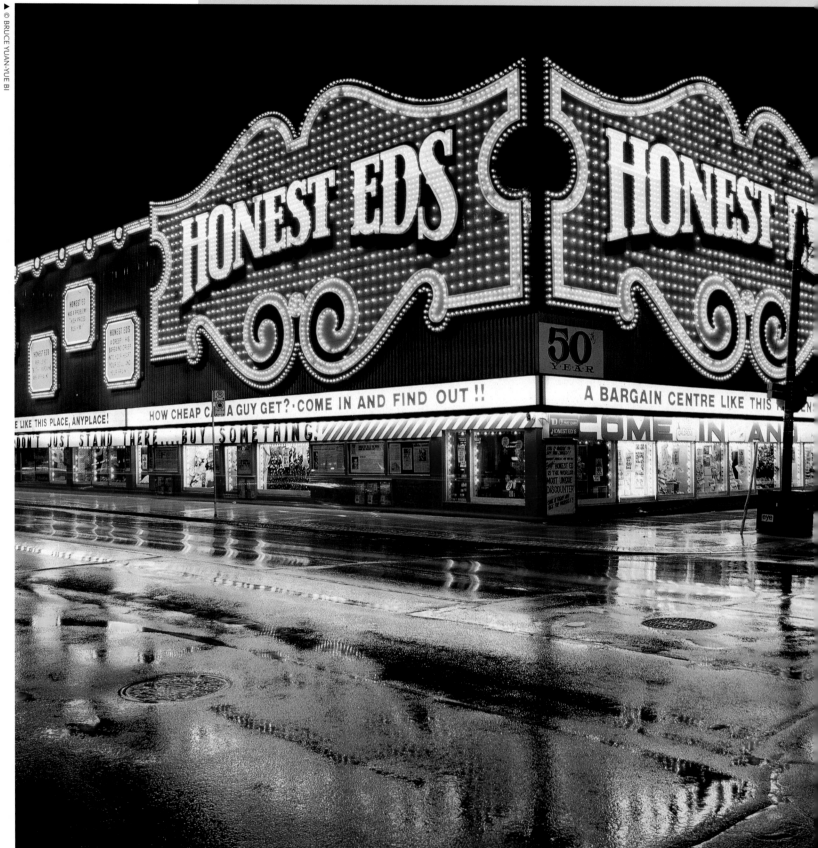

▲ © BRUCE YUAN-YUE BI

food from around the world, thanks in part to the many different cultures that have found a home here. There are even many ethnic areas—part of Danforth Avenue is Greek, for instance—that offer the best of international cuisine.

The desire to shop here is a long-standing trait, one that I'm proud to be associated with. Our retail store, Honest Ed's, started in the 1940s as The Sport Bar. It became and grew into Honest Ed's World Famous Bargain Shopping Centre more than 50 years ago, and has always stood as a one-of-a-kind retail operation that draws visitors from all over the world. The retail operation was declared a tourist landmark on its 40th anniversary.

© BRANDON KLAYMAN

Adjoining Honest Ed's on Markham Street, my family has acquired the houses on both sides of the street running south from Bloor Street to Lennox Street. The city has honoured us by naming this block Mirvish Village, home of more than 100 studios where artists practice painting, sculpture, woodcarving, jewellery making, and all types of arts and crafts. Mirvish Village will remain a place where no chain stores or big businesses are allowed to rent space, thereby offering the individual artists a place to pursue their dreams and realize their talents.

My wife, Anne, has a studio on the street, where she has sculpted dignitaries such as former Lieutenant-Governor Lincoln Alexander. In past years, my wife did the portrait of Supreme Court Justice Honourable Keiller McKay. This bronze portrait is now in the reception lounge at the Royal Alexandra Theatre. Mirvish Village is also the location of David Mirvish Books on Art. This is one of

© BRUCE YUAN-YUE BI

TORONTO

THE VIEW FROM THE TORONTO Harbour may have changed a bit in the last 100 years, but it is no less compelling and magical to visitors and locals alike.

◄ © FRANCO ROSSI

© FRANCO ROSSI

ORONTO HARBOUR IS THE best possible place to be on one of the city's legendarily muggy summer days, with all manner of watercraft available for lessons or cruising. From rowing to yachting to the Island Ferry, there's always a cool breeze for boaters on the lake.

▲ © BRUCE YUAN-YUE BI

© FRANCO ROSSI

WATER SEEMS TO INVITE city gatherings, particularly in summer. The boulevard of University Avenue (OPPOSITE TOP), the Alexander the Great parkette in the Danforth neighborhood (OPPOSITE BOTTOM), and the calm pool outside Roy Thomson Hall (LEFT) provide little oases in the concrete jungle.

▲ © FRANCO ROSSI

© FRANCO ROSSI

THE WACKY MIX OF OLD and new is what makes the urban centre of Toronto so interesting to explore. St. Andrews Presbyterian Church (BOTTOM LEFT), built in 1878, stands cheek by jowl with the ultramodern condominiums of Symphony Place—and the shining tower of Metro Hall is but a stone's throw from the 19th-century vintage storefronts of King Street (OPPOSITE). Sam the Record Man (LEFT), a fixture on Yonge Street since vinyl was king, now sells CDs and DVDs.

© FRANCO ROSSI

© FRANCO ROSSI

© DAVID JOHNS / HOT SHOTS STOCK SHOTS, INC.

FREQUENTLY PHOTOGRAPHED, the wedge-shaped Flatiron Building stands downtown in the triangle formed by Front, Church, and Wellington streets. Built in 1892 as the head office of the Gooderham and Worts Distillery, the building still has—and uses—its original elevator.

© BRUCE YUAN-YUE BI

© WINSTON FRASER

THREE OF THE MOST STRIKING buildings on the Toronto skyline are close neighbours to one another. The Royal Bank Tower (TOP) gleams, thanks to the 2,500 ounces of pure gold that adorn its 14,000 windows. Reflected in the gilded facade are the ultramodern towers of BCE Place (BOTTOM), just across the street. The landmark Royal York Hotel (OPPOSITE), which opened in 1929, was once the largest building in the British Empire.

© JAN BUTCHOFSKY-HOUSER / HOUSERSTOCK, INC.

© WINSTON FRASER

© RICHARD QUATAERT PHOTOGRAPHY

© RICHARD QUATAERT PHOTOGRAPHY

© WINSTON FRASER

Without a doubt, the most prominent buildings in the downtown core are banks, banks, banks. The largest of the Canadian chartered banks, all headquartered within a few small blocks around Bay Street, have a powerful impact on both the economy and the landscape. On a fine day, you can see clear across the lake to Buffalo, New York, from these pinnacles of finance.

▼ © FRANCO ROSSI

▼ © BRUCE YUAN-YUE BI

© FRANCO ROSSI

EVERY WEEK, MORE THAN 1 million people flock to Eaton's Centre, the famous glass-atriumed mall (LEFT). While the shops bustle during the day, students and researchers comb the shelves at the Metro Reference Library (OPPOSITE BOTTOM) for knowledge bargains.

© FRANCO ROSSI

THE WORLD WITHIN A CITY

© EMMANUEL VALCHER

© EMMANUEL VAUCHER

THE STREET LIFE OF TORONTO is as varied as its 4.5 million residents, many of whom come out on sunny days to enjoy the weather and such sights as the landmark Flatiron Building, which boasts a trompe l'oeil by Derek Besant (OPPOSITE). The three centre windows are real, but all the others were invented by the mind and hand of the artist.

© FRANCO ROSSI

© FRANCO ROSSI

THE WORLD WITHIN A CITY

© FRANCO ROSSI

▲ © JONATHAN POSTAL / TOWERY PUBLISHING, INC.

© JONATHAN POSTAL / TOWERY PUBLISHING, INC.

© JONATHAN POSTAL / TOWERY PUBLISHING, INC.

TORONTONIANS ARE FRIENDLY whether whizzing along Yonge Street, greeting guests at the Hotel International on Bloor Street, or just hanging out downtown. Some even extend a hand of friendship toward the city's ubiquitous pigeons.

▼ © BRANDON KLAYMAN

© FRANCO ROSSI

O N THE FIRST WARM DAY of the year, locals make a habit of eating lunch outside, and continue to do so until the weather becomes too unbearably cold. The phenomenon transcends cultural divides to include suited bureaucrats and politicians at City Hall and funky-haired denizens of Kensington Market. Not to be outdone, the high-powered people of Bay Street take a break from the bulls and the bears of the market to spend a little quality time in the calming presence of cast-iron cows (PAGES 52 AND 53).

▲ © BRAD CROOKS

▲ © BRAD CROOKS

© MARK WILSON

WATCH YOUR STEP, FOLKS: overlooking the popular Nathan Phillips Square skating rink in front of City Hall is one of Toronto's many moose sculptures. Underneath the rink and the Square is one of the largest and most complex parking lots in the city—one that requires an equally complex animal-based coding system for parking areas.

© FRANCO ROSSI

© FRANCO ROSSI

© FRANCO ROSSI

THEY SAY NO TWO SNOW-flakes are the same—and the same is true about Toronto's native moose. Commissioned by corporations and decorated by Canadian artists, the Moose in the City project was most popular with children and visitors. Before garnering some $1.2 million, however, the moose were endangered: souvenir hunters made a nasty habit of absconding with their antlers.

© FRANCO ROSSI

SOMEONE TO WATCH OVER me: Torontonians look out for one another, as the city's statuary reflects. From Foo Dogs to Santa Claus-clothed moose, a full spectrum of creatures may be pressed into service as guardian angels.

© FRANCO ROSSI

© BRUCE YUAN-YUE BI

IN A CITY WHERE ART ENJOYS an ongoing renaissance, local artists provide a veritable cornucopia of talent. From the sidewalks of Queen Street (LEFT) to the brick walls of the St. Lawrence Market (OPPOSITE), every surface offers a potential canvas.

▲ © RICHARD QUATAERT PHOTOGRAPHY

▲ © JUDY NISENHOLT

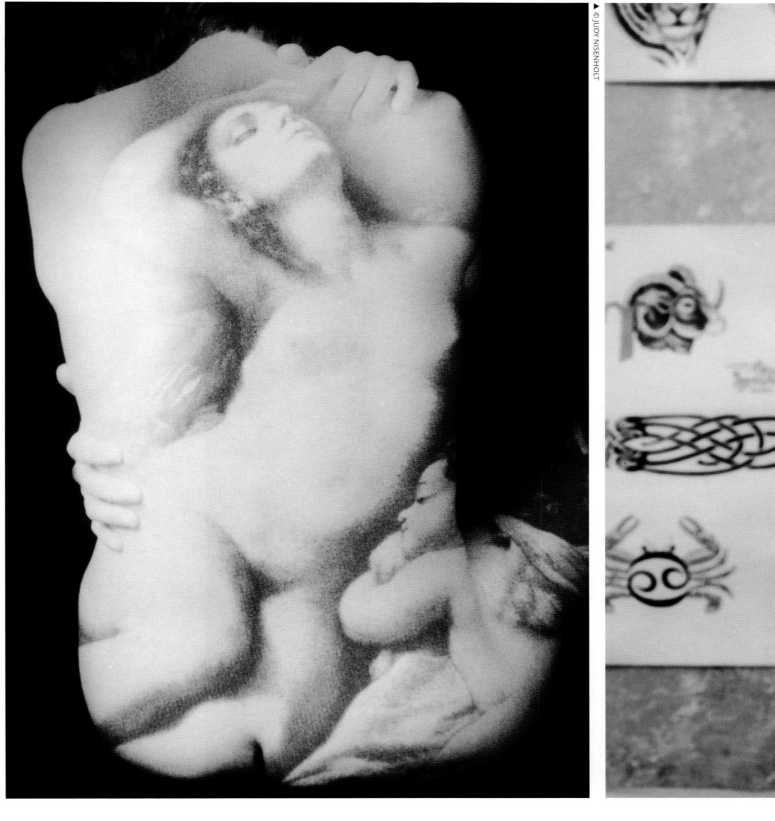

PRINTING : BY HAND MA

TORONTO IS THE CAPITAL OF
the arts in English Canada
and a noted centre for
Canadian art, much overlooked in
the United States and Europe. The
body too is a canvas for Toronto
artists and artisans, as it offers a
myriad of ways for using it both
temporarily and permanently.

A MINIMUM OF COMMITMENT—
but a maximum of creativity—
go into the city's transient
artistic efforts. Sign painters are
always in demand in the theatre
district, where—over the course
of a year—dozens of productions
come and go. Henna tattoos
from Kensington Market provide
contemporary adornment without
requiring intergenerational
explanations.

© BRAD CROOKS

F ROM THREE-D TO GRAFFITI to entreaty, brightly embel-lished walls throughout Toronto appeal to the eye and draw viewers to the businesses marked by creative exteriors.

© SKULL FOR HOLD

© MARK WILSON

© MARK WILSON

Nearly two-thirds of Toronto's residents were born and raised elsewhere, creating a virtual United Nations of cultural backgrounds. One result of this mix is a plethora of ethnic neighbourhoods—such as Little India (LEFT), any of the city's several Chinatowns (OPPOSITE TOP), and Little Italy (OPPOSITE BOTTOM)—each rich with residences, restaurants, and shops.

© DAVID JOHNS / HOT SHOTS STOCK SHOTS, INC.

© BORIS SPREMO, C.M.

© DAVID JOHNS / HOT SHOTS STOCK SHOTS, INC.

© BRANDON KLAYMAN

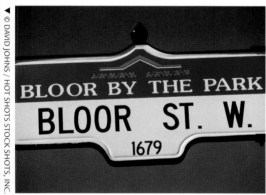

© DAVID JOHNS / HOT SHOTS STOCK SHOTS, INC.

© BRUCE YUAN-YUE BI

NEIGHBOURHOOD-PROUD
local business associations
employ customized signs
and other decorative work to enhance
their streetscapes. The extraordinary

"Honest Ed" and Anne Mirvish
(OPPOSITE CENTRE) reign supreme
over the city's theatre district—
one block of which is aptly named
Mirvish Walkway.

© JONATHAN POSTAL / TOWERY PUBLISHING, INC.

▲ © DAVE HOUSER/ HOUSERSTOCK, INC.

NE OF THE GREATEST advantages of a multicultural city is the resultant ability to visit dozens of countries without a passport—and without even leaving town.

▲ © JUDY NISENHOLT

▲ © JONATHAN POSTAL / TOWERY PUBLISHING, INC.

© DAVE HOUSER/ HOUSERSTOCK, INC.

KENSINGTON MARKET WAS born in the early 1900s, as recent Russian, Polish, and Jewish immigrants began setting up produce stalls in front of their homes. Since its inception, the area has been one of the best places in the city to get the biggest bargains and freshest food from the most crowded streets. By the mid-1970s, Kensington's western boundary had formed another vibrant and busy neighbourhood: Chinatown.

© DAVE HOUSER/ HOUSERSTOCK INC.

© DAVE HOUSER / HOUSERSTOCK INC.

S HOPPING FOR ANTIQUES
in Toronto runs the full
price-point gamut, from the
adventure of separating gems from
junk on Queen Street to the "mink
mile" of nearly priceless finds in
upscale Yorkville.

ONCE THE LONG, COLD winter ends, shopping outside becomes an urban obsession. The vintage clothing shops of Kensington Market (TOP AND OPPOSITE) can stretch their out-door display of wares for nearly the entire year, but that's a luxury not afforded to the less-protected—but equally popular—jewellery vendors of Queen Street West (BOTTOM).

▼ © JONATHAN POSTAL / TOWERY PUBLISHING, INC.

© JONATHAN POSTAL / TOWERY PUBLISHING, INC.

© BRUCE YUAN-YUE BI

B EING IN THE PINK IS MUCH more chic than being in the red. The rosy trend could be accredited to Kingi Carpenter (OP-POSITE LEFT), whose one-of-a-kind clothes boutique on Queen Street West—Peach Berserk Cocktails—has long been ablaze with eye-catching, head-turning, hotter-than-hot pink.

▼ © DAVE GREEN

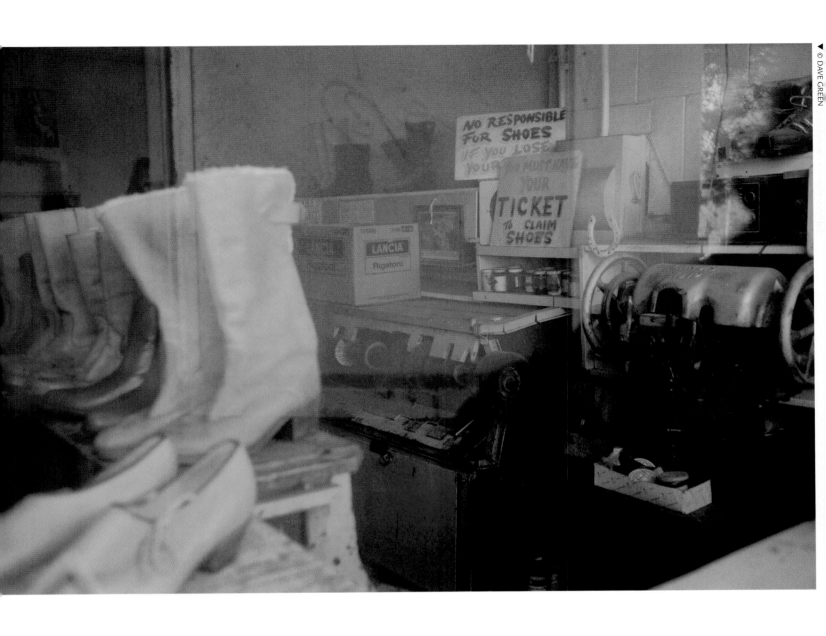

▲ © JAN BUTCHOFSKY-HOUSER / HOUSERSTOCK, INC.

T HESE BOOTS WERE MADE for walking—or for skating. Cobblers can still be found in some corners of the city, helping keep Torontonians covered from heel to toe.

© BRAD CROOKS

"Ginger" Spice

These shoes were worn by former Spice Girl Geri Halliwell, otherwise known as "Ginger" Spice. The Bata Shoe Museum purchased four pairs of Halliwell's boots and shoes at a charity auction in 1998, including a pair of "Union Jack" platforms worn in the 1998 movie *Spice World*. Halliwell has recently been appointed by the United Nations as an ambassador of women's issues.

GINGER SPICE

© BRANDON KLEIMAN

© JONATHAN POSTAL / TOWERY PUBLISHING, INC.

Providing exercise for the mind and the feet, Toronto's fine museums explore some of the wonders and mysteries of the world. At the Ontario Science Centre (LEFT), visitors investigate and interact with the magic of space, technology, and communications. The Bata Shoe Museum (OPPOSITE) maintains a collection of more than 10,000 items of footwear.

© ANNE LEVENSTON / KLIX

© MARK WILSON

F ROM PARADES TO PUNK, self-expression runs rampant in Toronto. Each year, the local gay pride march (ABOVE) draws revellers from around the region. On the musical front, the group Serial Joe (OPPOSITE) produces pointed lyrics for its enthusiastic fans.

© STEVE EPRILE / HOT SHOTS STOCK SHOTS, INC.

© MARK WILSON

© FRANCO ROSSI

FROM THE 553-METRE-TALL CN Tower (ABOVE) to the Old City Hall (OPPOSITE RIGHT)— one of the city's tallest structures when it was built in 1899—the sky's the limit for some of Toronto's most famous buildings—and for a number of locals, too.

© FRANCO ROSSI

© BRAD CROOKS

V IEWING TORONTO FROM
the CN Tower, the tallest
free-standing structure in the
world, is very similar to observing
the city from the cockpit of a
helicopter. The trip in the tower's
high-speed, glass-fronted elevators
is the quicker of the two: the ride
to the LookOut level takes less
than a minute.

◆ © FRANCO ROSSI

ORONTO'S SKYLINE IS
studded with steel and
spiked with skyscrapers—
and occasionally awash in acrobats,
who find that the fun of flying
mitigates the fear of falling.

STREETCARS HAVE LONG been a part of the Toronto landscape—and airspace. The first electric streetcar, heated by coal stoves, made its inaugural trip in 1892. Now, almost 250 streetcars on 11 routes whiz across the city, carrying passengers to destinations throughout the downtown core.

OARING STONE AND LUSH landscaping mark the graceful entrances of many of Toronto's structures, from Queen's Park—home to the Ontario Legislature (TOP)—to the Royal Ontario Museum (BOTTOM LEFT), Holy Blossom Temple (BOTTOM RIGHT), and Osgoode Hall (OPPOSITE), originally built to house the Law Society of Upper Canada.

© BRANDON KLAYMAN

© CITY OF TORONTO ARCHIVES, SC 497, ITEM 124

© BORIS SPREMO, C.M.

THE BUILDING NOW KNOWN as Old City Hall is actually the third of Toronto's city halls. Designed by renowned architect of the day E.J. Lennox and completed in 1899, the landmark was declared a National Historic Site by the Historic Sites and Monuments Board of Canada in 1989.

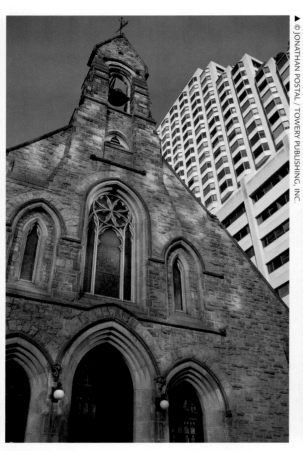

© JONATHAN POSTAL / TOWERY PUBLISHING, INC.

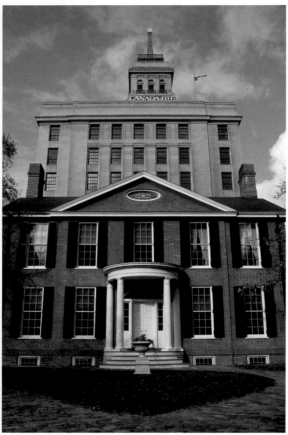

TORONTO'S ARCHITECTURE is as varied as its populace. From the neo-Gothic arches of the Church of the Redeemer (TOP LEFT) on Bloor Street to the stately Georgian symmetry of Campbell House (TOP RIGHT), and from the sleek, streamlined moderne Design Exchange—formerly the Toronto Stock Exchange—(BOTTOM) to the Romanesque revival-style Victoria College (OPPOSITE), the city has a strong foundation in its historic buildings.

© BRANDON KLAYMAN

© JONATHAN POSTAL / TOWERY PUBLISHING, INC.

THE MAJESTY OF A CLASSIC arch is unrivalled, wherever it appears and however it is decorated. A well-rounded selection of inspired examples appears throughout Toronto, including the ornate Old City Hall (TOP LEFT), the beautiful Lillian H. Smith branch of the Toronto Public Library (TOP RIGHT), peaceful Mount Pleasant Cemetery (BOTTOM LEFT), and the Gooderham & Worts distillery (OPPOSITE).

© ANNE LEVENSTON / KLIX

© BRANDON KLAYMAN

Top o' the Senator
BRIAN DICKINSON
LIVE JAZZ UPSTAIRS

Toronto's musical hot spots strike the right note for many listeners in Toronto. The city's first club devoted exclusively to jazz—Top o' the Senator (ABOVE) on Victoria Street—and legendary blues club Grossman's Tavern on Spading Avenue (OPPOSITE) appeal to devotees and curious newcomers alike.

© BRANDON KLAYMAN

THE TORONTO-BASED BLUE Rodeo, led by singer Greg Keelor (LEFT), has been producing hits for more than two decades. Though most of the members of The Tragically Hip hail from Kingston, Ontario, lead singer and Toronto resident Gord Downie (OPPOSITE) is one of the local music scene's most popular performers.

© FRANCO ROSSI

TAKING IT TO THE STREETS: up-and-coming musicians can often be found performing outside in this street-lively city—although they may occasionally need to compete with the much rarer sight of a troupe of dancers for spectators' attention.

THE WORLD WITHIN A CITY

TAKING IT TO THE STREETS: up-and-coming musicians can often be found performing outside in this street-lively city—although they may occasionally need to compete with the much rarer sight of a troupe of dancers for spectators' attention.

© JONATHAN POSTAL / TOWERY PUBLISHING, INC.

Actors, artisans, and athletes, whether in or out of costume, all leave their marks on Toronto. At historic Fort York (LEFT), which underwent extensive renovations in 2000, staff members provide a glimpse into life during the early 19th century, and also reenactment battles from the War of 1812. Bowmaker Christian Wanka (RIGHT) gives virtuoso performances, plying his delicate craft. Born in India, Tiger Jeet Singh (OPPOSITE) now lives in Milton, just north of Toronto. Singh has been wrestling in his adopted country since the 1960s, and he was named a WWA World Martial Arts champion in 1992.

T HE CANADIAN NATIONAL Exhibition (CNE) began in 1879, primarily as an agricultural event. Now an annual extravaganza of rides, games, and shows attracting millions of attendees each year, the CNE hits the city like a tidal wave in mid-August and recedes again on Labour Day (PAGES 122-125).

© PAUL TILL/ KLIX

© FRANCO ROSSI

T HE SPRAWLING ENTERTAIN-
ment complex known as
The Docks is just one of
many east-end harbourfront attractions. It boasts a 41,000-square-foot
lakeside patio, swimming pool,
beach volleyball court, and other
recreational opportunities.

© FRANCO ROSSI

With its numerous cycling lanes and paved cycling trails, Toronto sometimes seems to be a two-wheeled city. Whether on a snowy slope at Riverdale Park (ABOVE) or a sandy shore on Centre Island (OPPOSITE), cyclists can test their pedal mettle year-round.

THE TORONTO ISLANDS
are a chain of eight small,
car-free land masses that
have been attracting visitors since
the mid-19th century. Centre Island,
the largest of the group, is accessible
by ferry and boasts gardens, games,
and "Please walk on the grass" signs.

THE 14TH-LARGEST FRESH-water lake in the world, Lake Ontario now serves as Toronto's sole source of drinking water. Onshore, the lakefront is a tranquil place to walk, or simply to relax and enjoy the view.

◆ © BRAD CROOKS

KNOWN AS THE BEACH OR The Beaches, this water-front neighbourhood is a little slice of California in Toronto. The boardwalk is shaded by huge, graceful trees, and the area stretches from Leslie Street to the rocky shore by the R.C. Harris Water Filtration Plant.

141

© BRANDON KLAYMAN

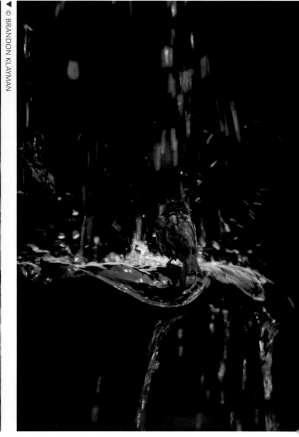

ANIMAL KINGDOM: SINCE
its opening in August 1974,
the not-for-profit Metro
Toronto Zoo (LEFT AND OPPOSITE,
BOTTOM LEFT) has delighted more
than 30 million guests. There are
more than 5,000 inhabitants at the
zoo, representing some 450 species.

HE WORLD WITHIN A CITY

VICTORIAN ARCHITECTURE, replete with ornate decoration, dominates downtown Toronto's neighbourhoods. Many of these houses were restored and renovated in the 1970s, when urban professionals began to see the value in living so close to their workplaces. Some of the classic Victorian sections of town include Kensington Market (BOTTOM LEFT), Yorkville (BOTTOM RIGHT), and Cabbagetown (OPPOSITE).

© RICHARD QUATAERT PHOTOGRAPHY

HISTORY IS OPEN TO THE public in Toronto. At the Royal Ontario Museum (TOP), visitors can view re-created tableaux of historical rooms. Spadina House, on the crest of Spadina Hill (BOTTOM), was built in 1866 and is filled with the art and artifacts of the James Austin family. Next door (OPPOSITE) is the grandiose Casa Loma, now a museum of architectural styles, with each room featuring a different one.

THE ART GALLERY OF Ontario is probably most famous for the Henry Moore Sculpture Centre, which houses the world's largest public collection of Moore's work (ABOVE).

The gallery's Canadian Historical Collection (OPPOSITE) includes major works by some of Canada's greatest painters, including Carr, Krieghoff, Milne, and Watson.

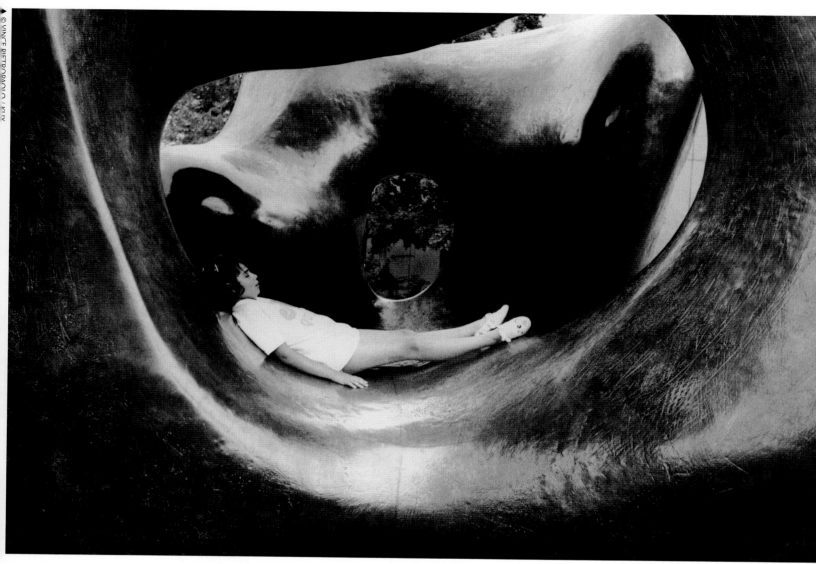

© VINCE PIETROPAOLO / KLIX

GETTING INTO ART MEANS different things to different people. For some, it means succumbing to temptation and crawling inside the Henry Moores outside the Art Gallery of Ontario. For others, like artist Milena Tomic, it means creating performances for actors and audiences alike.

◆ © CRAIG MELVIN / ALLSPORT

157

Seventh-inning stretch: the Toronto Blue Jays won consecutive World Series in 1992 and 1993. They can be found warming up toward a repeat of those performances from April to September at SkyDome.

F ROM ANY ANGLE, BLUE JAYS fans of all casts have a great view—particularly when the SkyDome's roof is open, revealing the CN Tower in all its glory.

© ZORAN MILICH / ALLSPORT

Toronto Maple Leaf hockey fans are nurtured from an early age and quickly become dedicated for life. The Leafs have made it to nearly 20 Stanley Cup playoffs, and have taken home 10 of the coveted cups. As the season is nearly always completely sold out in advance, hockey tickets are notoriously hard to come by.

THE TORONTO ARGONAUTS—nicknamed the Boatmen—have a storied history that goes back to 1873, when the team was founded by the Argonaut Rowing Club. Fans today, however, focus primarily on the pigskin and cheer themselves blue for the Argos.

THE CITY'S NBA FRANCHISE, the Toronto Raptors, had its inaugural season in 1995. The Raptors Dance Pack entertains the crowd in between such game highlights as forward Antonio Davis slamming down an emphatic deuce.

THE HEART-THUMPING
excitement of the races can
be experienced just 30 minutes north of the city at Woodbine
racetrack, one of Canada's premier
showplaces of Thoroughbred and
harness racing (TOP AND BOTTOM
RIGHT). Outside the track, a statue
of the legendary Native Dancer
provides inspiration and dreams
for jockeys like Robert Landry
(BOTTOM LEFT). Offering a slightly
different thrill, the annual Santa
Claus Parade (OPPOSITE) lassos
spectators with its floats and
costumed marchers.

© JONATHAN POSTAL / TOWERY PUBLISHING, INC.

CREATED IN 1967, TORONTO'S Caribana has grown into one of North America's largest cultural festivals. With its steel drum banks and brilliant dress, the annual, multiweek party attracts people from all over the hemisphere and has brought more than $4 billion into the city's economy.

© DAVID GRIFFITH

THE OPEN-AIR MARKETS OF Chinatown and Kensington are reminiscent of times past. The markets are dense, bustling, and fragrant—and the food, as everyone knows, is simply out of this world.

IN ADDITION TO THE CUISINE offered by Chinatown's restaurants, the fish vendors at Toronto's open-air markets are legendary as some of the city's best sources of inexpensive, fresh fish and seafood. Gourmets all over town have preferred spots where they can pick up everything from sea bass to marlin steaks.

© MARK WILSON

T HE BRIGHT LIGHTS IN this big city illuminate everything from dance emporiums and music clubs to ice-cream parlours and neighbourhood cafés.

© VINCE PIETROPAOLO / KLIX

PROFILES IN EXCELLENCE

A LOOK AT THE CORPORATIONS, BUSINESSES, PROFESSIONAL GROUPS, AND COMMUNITY SERVICE ORGANIZATIONS THAT HAVE MADE THIS BOOK POSSIBLE. THEIR STORIES—OFFERING AN INFORMAL CHRONICLE OF THE LOCAL BUSINESS COMMUNITY—ARE ARRANGED ACCORDING TO THE DATE THEY WERE ESTABLISHED IN THE TORONTO AREA.

ADC Software Systems Canada Ltd.

Adecco Employment Services Limited ✤ ADP Canada

AGF Management Limited ✤ Airport Group Canada Inc.

AllCanada Express Limited

Alliance Atlantis Communications, Inc.

The Alliance Personnel Group Inc. ✤ Anixter Canada Inc.

Biovail Corporation ✤ Blake, Cassels & Graydon LLP

Boeing Toronto Ltd. ✤ Bombardier Aerospace

The Cadillac Fairview Corporation Limited

The Canadian Institute of Chartered Accountants

CanWest Global Communications Corp.

Chubb Insurance Company of Canada ✤ CHUM Limited

Cole, Sherman & Associates Limited ✤ Courtesy Chev Olds Ltd.

Deep Foundations Contractors Inc. ✤ Delfour Corporation

Fogler, Rubinoff LLP ✤ Goodman and Carr LLP

Greater Toronto Airports Authority ✤ Holiday Inn On King

Homag Canada Inc. ✤ Honeywell ✤ Humber College

LCBO ✤ Marsh Canada Limited ✤ Metrus Properties Limited

Molson Canada ✤ NLnovalink ✤ The Old Mill Inn

Ontario Power Generation ✤ Ontario Teachers' Pension Plan Board

Rex Pak Limited ✤ The Riverdale Hospital

S&C Electric Canada Ltd. ✤ St. John's Rehabilitation Hospital

The Scarborough Hospital ✤ Scotiabank

Seneca College of Applied Arts and Technology

Sun Life Financial ✤ Teknion Corporation

Teranet Inc. ✤ Tim Hortons

The Toronto Board of Trade/World Trade Centre Toronto

Toronto French School ✤ The Toronto Star ✤ Trebor Personnel Inc.

The Westin Harbour Castle ✤ Wilson Logistics, Inc.

W. T. Lynch Foods Limited ✤ Xerox Canada Ltd.

Yorkton Securities Inc. ✤ Ziedler Grinnell Partnership / Architects

▲ © WINSTON FRASER

TORONTO

1786
1920

OLSON CANADA WAS FOUNDED BY JOHN MOLSON IN 1786, when Canada was not yet a country and the United States was less than 10 years old. Back then, there was no refrigeration. And, since the quality of brewing good beer depends on controlling the temperature of the

fermenter, Molson only brewed beer from November through March, and produced just over 4,000 gallons each year. He would cut ice blocks out of the St. Lawrence River and store the beer in subterranean vaults below the ground, using this natural refrigeration to keep the beer cold. To this day, those old vaults are still visible under the company's Montreal brewery.

Things have changed in the more than 215 years since the company was founded. Today, Molson is North America's oldest beer brand name and Canada's pre-eminent brewer, producing billions of gallons each year, with more than $2 billion in annual sales. Molson has remained, through all that time, a family company. Eric H. Molson, the great-great-great-grandson of John Molson, is chairman of the board, and many other Molson family members have also worked at the company, both past and present.

John Molson founded Molson Canada in 1786 when Canada was not yet a country and the United States was less than 10 years old.

A TRADITION OF BREWING

With breweries in Edmonton, Montreal, Regina, St. John's, Toronto, and Vancouver, Molson is able to draw on the best brewmasters in the country. Molson's intense focus on the brewing process has made the Molson portfolio of beers among the most famous—not only in Canada, but around the world.

Many of these well-known and high-profile brands, such as Molson Canadian, Molson Export, Coors Light, Molson Dry, and Rickard's Red, along with Molson-imported Corona and Heineken, are market leaders in their categories. Molson is the leading seller of all ale, lager, dry, and light beers sold in Canada.

Molson's dedication and unparalleled commitment to quality are what make Molson one of the best beers in the country. Every morning, at each Molson brewery around the country, highly trained tasters sample the beer, paying special attention to minute variations in beer flavour and aroma. The tasters must give their approval before any beer leaves the brewery. When new products are introduced, large teams of consumers are given samples to determine the new product's potential popularity. When there are significant changes in suppliers of ingredients, additional tasting teams are assembled to ensure consistency.

"RANT"ING AND RAVING ABOUT MOLSON

Molson is a favourite with beer drinkers across the country, and has secured and reinforced its position by continually creating great advertisements. Molson's advertisements always cause a sensation and create chatter on the street and in newsrooms. Molson Canadian's highly successful I AM Canadian campaign produced "The Rant," one

Many of Molson's well-known and high-profile brands are market leaders in their categories.

Molson's intense focus on the brewing process has made the company's portfolio of beers among the most famous—not only in Canada, but around the world.

the most successful TV commercials in Canadian history.

Fans across the country were glued to their TV sets watching Joe Canadian rant about why he's so proud to be Canadian. Joe delivered his rant live at hockey and football games, at concerts, and on Parliament Hill. Joe Canadian even travelled across Canada on Canada Day, visiting 10 cities in 28 hours and delivering the rant to wild and appreciative crowds decked out in red and white. Fans were so enamoured of the commercial that they even made up their own rants and had them published in newspapers and on Web sites.

MOLSON IN TORONTO

In a city of more than 2 million people, Molson has made a lasting impression in Toronto. In 1952, Molson announced it would build a $1.2 million, state-of-the-art brewery near Toronto's Canadian National Exhibition. Two years later, the Fleet Street Brewery opened with a gigantic, five-day celebration for employees, visiting dignitaries, and the public. The brewery produced Molson's first lager, Crown and Anchor, and all beers produced at the plant were sold across North America.

A lesser-known Molson Toronto landmark is the former Molson's Bank on Queen Street in Toronto's west end. The bank was part of an early Molson family venture into

financial services—one with its own currency. While the bank has long since been closed, its sign remains as a reminder of Molson's history in the city.

In February 1999, Mayor Mel Lastman introduced the megacity's newest citizen—Toronto's Own Amber Lager, a new beer brewed by Molson

available within Toronto city limits. Toronto's Own is a craft-brewed, 5.1-percent-alcohol-by-volume lager with an inviting amber colour and a pleasant hint of maple, giving it a strong Canadian identity. And, after only a few years in existence, Toronto's Own has quickly become the toast of the town.

Joe Canadian became part of Molson Canada's highly successful I AM Canadian campaign, ranting about why he's proud to be Canadian.

MOLSON SCORES WITH SPORTS FANS

Molson has been involved with sports for many decades, dating back to a time when there were only six teams in the National Hockey League and long before the National Basketball Association expanded north of the Canadian/U.S. border.

Molson's newest brewery in Ontario is located in the heart of every sports fan's fantasy. When the Air Canada Centre came to fruition, it seemed only fitting that Molson should be a part of the Toronto Maple Leafs' and Toronto Raptors' winning lineups. Located on the concourse level of the Air Canada Centre, adjacent to the sports bar, Rickard's Brewhouse is visible to the public and produces more than 600,000 bottles of beer (25,000 cases) each year.

For generations, Molson has been one of the largest supporters of Canadian hockey. Molson is the main sponsor of all six Canadian NHL teams, and also has a strong relationship with the Canadian Hockey Association. Molson is particularly proud of its association with hockey at the grass-roots level and its commitment to thousands of community hockey teams across the country.

In 1999, Molson sponsored the Open Ice Hockey Summit, which brought together some of the best minds in professional and amateur hockey. The world-renowned conference examined and sought ways to

Joe Canadian delivers his rant live at hockey games.

Together with the House of Blues Canada, Molson presents more than 800 shows a year in venues such as Molson Amphitheatre in Toronto.

improve the way the game is taught and played in Canada.

Molson is also heavily involved in one of the most exciting motor sports events in North America—the Molson Indy, which takes place in Toronto every July and in Vancouver every September. This stop on the Indy circuit attracts the best drivers in the world, including Canadian favourites such as Paul Tracy and Patrick Carpentier.

In addition to hockey and auto racing, Molson also supports football, slo-pitch, golf, boating, volleyball, and lacrosse, to name just a few.

SINGING MOLSON'S PRAISES

Molson's association with music in Canada is legendary, and the company has become a driving force in entertainment. Together with the House of Blues Canada, Molson presents more than 800 shows a year in venues such as Molson Amphitheatre in Toronto, Molson Park in Barrie, and Molson Centre in Montreal—three of the best venues for seeing the world's most exciting concerts. Cultural icons, including Bob Dylan and the Guess Who, as well as younger

talents like Britney Spears and Beck have been a part of Molson's top-notch musical productions.

Molson is very involved with Edgefest, an annual concert event that brings some of the newest and most popular names in music to major outdoor concerts in several cities across Canada each summer. Always looking for ways to promote Canada's up-and-coming musicians, Molson included a compilation CD featuring the country's most promising young talent, in cases of Molson Canadian in summer 2000.

The Molson Canadian Rocks program has brought the best in music to Canadians for more than 10 years. Molson Canadian Rocks Simulbase was the major music festival in 2000, bringing more than 40,000 Canadians together on Canada Day from coast to coast. Five live Molson concerts, featuring some of the world's biggest bands, took place in five cities across the country in one night. A satellite feed connected all the venues in real time so fans across Canada got to see all five concerts. Over the years, Molson Canadian Rocks has staged many memorable bashes, including the Join The Party Canada Day concert, Blind Date concert

series, Cabin Parties, and Embassy concert in London, England, starring Jimmy Page and Robert Plant.

THE MOLSON COMMUNITY

Although Molson is a growing global brewer, the company acts locally in every significant way. John Molson believed that everyone had to play his or her part in making communities better. That philosophy has been passed down from generation to generation at Molson. Playing a leadership role in communities across Canada has been as much a part of the Molson tradition as making beer.

Molson supports a variety of causes and charities through the Molson Donation Fund (MDF), made up of Molson employees who keep the fund in touch with local needs. MDF supports organizations in health and social welfare, education, the arts, and the environment.

Molson's nationwide Local Heroes program grants funding to individuals looking to fix up existing sports and recreational facilities in their community. The Local Heroes program began in 1997 and has made a difference by funding thousands of projects across the country.

Molson is also well known for its ongoing involvement in community events, such as Toronto's Beaches Jazz Festival, AIDS Committee, and a

variety of charities. Molson encourages its employees to volunteer their time and get involved in local service clubs, as well as helping out local charitable organizations.

Nationally, Molson is committed to the responsible use of alcohol, and has run a number of advertising campaigns that focus on drinking and driving and the need to plan ahead.

Environmental leadership is another of Molson's key community activities. The company works with

other brewers in creating the recycling program at the Beer Store in Ontario, one of the most effective and efficient re-use and reclamation systems in the world. With a very small incentive, beer drinkers are encouraged to return their empty beer bottles, cans, cases, and caps, which are then returned to the breweries for sterilization and re-use.

Tradition and heritage are two qualities that are very important to Molson Canada. The company is passionate about being Canadian and is proud to remain 100 percent Canadian owned. The Molson family's commitment to creating world-renowned beers has continued for more than 215 years and has created a company that is very much a part of the Canadian heritage. 🍁

Molson's dedication and unparalleled commitment to quality makes Molson one of the best beers in the country (left).

Hop vines grow to a height of more than 4.5 metres and their dried flower clusters give Molson's beer its refreshing tang (right).

Located on the concourse level of the Air Canada Centre, adjacent to the sports bar, Rickard's Brewhouse is visible to the public. It produces more than 600,000 bottles of beer (25,000 cases) each year.

AS DIVERSE AND WIDE-RANGING AS THE CITY ITSELF, THE TORONTO Board of Trade/World Trade Centre Toronto has been representing the business community in Toronto since 1845. With an active membership spread throughout Toronto and the Greater Toronto Area, it remains the largest community business organization and chamber of commerce in Canada.

Funded entirely by the private sector, the Board strives to build a better community through business leadership. Its volunteers and staff achieve this goal by providing various business services; advocating public policy positions with the federal, provincial, and municipal governments; participating in community partnerships; and facilitating economic and business development.

COMPETING GLOBALLY, MEETING LOCALLY

The Board offers its members all of the necessary tools to compete successfully on a global scale. Further to this end, it operates three facilities in the Toronto area: the Downtown Centre, the Airport Centre, and the Golf & Country Club. Each centre provides members with the resources necessary to promote and conduct their business operations.

The Downtown Centre is located in the heart of Toronto's financial district at First Canadian Place. The centre features an executive restaurant, meeting rooms, and a comprehensive Resource Centre. The centre makes available the latest research

Dick Pound, a member of the International Olympic Committee, addresses members of the Toronto Board of Trade/World Trade Centre Toronto.

and resource materials busy executives may need, including books, periodicals, CD-ROMs, and the Internet.

For business meetings and travellers, the Airport Centre offers convenient meeting rooms, the Above Board restaurant, and banquet facilities. The centre can hold up to 250 people for meetings or dining,

depending on the configuration required by the client.

Located in Woodbridge, just outside Toronto, the Golf & Country Club offers recreational and business opportunities in a relaxed atmosphere. Visitors can play golf, toboggan, or ice-skate as the occasion and season allow. Meeting and dining rooms are available to members

Lemon Moose, part of Toronto's Moose in the City promotion, was purchased by past presidents of the Toronto Board of Trade. Pictured are (from left) D. Brown, J. Clarry, G. Meinzer, S. Edwards, J.D. Crashley. Missing from photo is G. Fierheller.

of the Board's organizational strength to facilitate economic development.

One tool to increase members' potential is the *Toronto Region Business and Market Guide,* an important research piece featuring economic profiles and local government guides, as well as information on vacancy rates, incomes, cost of living, real estate, and business distribution. The guide is an excellent resource for businesses in Greater Toronto and for those considering relocation to the area.

BRINGING CITY BUSINESSES TOGETHER

The Board continues to host functions that provide new opportunities for members to expand their contacts and knowledge. Influential guest speakers have included David Dodge, the newly appointed Governor of the Bank of Canada, making his first public address; businessman Ted Rogers; federal, provincial, and municipal leaders, including the Prime Minister and provincial premiers; the executives of certain Fortune 500 companies; and various international leaders from around the world. Speaker series are offered based on industry and office, and provide information and networking opportunities.

In the interest of promoting and strengthening trade and business development, the Board also arranges small, informal meetings between local businesspersons and visiting officials. Networking breakfasts and receptions allow existing members to meet newcomers, and provide an opportunity to build and expand on members' sets of contacts. The Board's famous annual dinner offers an occasion to network with clients, friends, and colleagues.

The Toronto Board of Trade/ World Trade Centre Toronto represents the voice of Greater Toronto's business community, reaching beyond the corporate bank towers to the smallest street retailer. With a membership as diverse as the city itself, the Board promotes events and policies that support economic development and growth. By working to make the business climate more favourable, the Board looks to create and cultivate a network of businesses and people dedicated to making Toronto a competitive, world-class city—and keeping it there. 🍁

A scenic view overlooking the Toronto Board of Trade's Golf & Country Club

year-round to help complete their day, whether focussed on business, pleasure, or both.

Worksite, the Board's business resource centre, is available at both the Downtown Centre and Golf & Country Club sites. It is a place to meet and work outside the office, helping busy executives stay in touch and make the best use of their time. At Worksite, an executive can book an office for the day, or by the hour, to meet with clients; access the Internet; or purchase publications on Toronto businesses. Worksite also allows workers to stay in touch with the office by phone, fax, or E-mail.

Another tool the Board utilizes for its members is the World Trade Centre, which is linked to 305 similar sites in 92 countries. When Toronto-area members travel overseas, they may take advantage of these centres for private dining and reception services. Back in Toronto, the International Trade Library in the Resource Centre contains an extensive reference collection. The Board also offers the Import/Export Certificate Program to assist businesses in identifying global market opportu-

nities, mastering foreign exchange theory, and learning the basics of global routing, packing, and marketing. By providing these services, the Board assists members in reaching broader and wider audiences throughout the world.

PROMOTING BUSINESS ACTIVISM

In order to promote a stronger and more competitive city, the Board takes positions on public policy and lobbies all levels of government. Committees and task forces involving business leaders develop policies on issues of concern to members and the business community at large. Some of these issues are property tax reform, education reform, economic development, local governance, and sustainable physical infrastructure. The committees and task forces look at what is best for the community, with an understanding that a healthy community is essential for a healthy business.

Another focus of the Board is business and economic development. Toward that end, it offers a variety of opportunities and services for members, allowing them to take advantage

OUNDED IN 1856, BLAKE, CASSELS & GRAYDON LLP PLAYS A LEADING role in Canada's legal and business communities. As one of the oldest and largest law firms in the country, Blakes, as it is known, has expertise in virtually every area of law affecting business. The firm's diverse client base includes many of North America's corporate

establishment as well as many of the so-called "new economy" businesses.

Blakes was founded by some of the leading lawyers practising at the time. Sir Edward Blake was a dominant political figure in Upper Canada, and was intimately involved in the region's growth into a modern nation. Partner Zebulon Aiton Lash helped create the precursor to the Canadian National Railways, which linked Canada from sea to sea. These two lawyers and other Blakes partners counseled the great capitalists and industrialists of early Canada, and built a tradition of business expertise and legal innovation that continues into the 21st century.

Today, Blakes has more than 440 lawyers in four Canadian offices in Toronto, Ottawa, Calgary, and Vancouver, and two international offices in London and Bejing. Dedicated to helping the firm's clients achieve their business objectives, Blakes prides itself on providing innovative, timely, and cost-effective legal advice.

Blake, Cassels & Graydon LLP has expertise in virtually every area of law affecting business. Through its memberships in international legal referral networks, the firm also has non-exclusive associations with major law firms in every industrialized nation and most developing countries.

EXPERTISE AND EXPERIENCE

Blakes is recognized both domestically and internationally for its expertise in all areas of legal practice affecting business, including corporate/securities law, litigation, financial services, real estate, restructuring and insolvency, intellectual property, pensions, and tax. During 2000, the firm worked on a number of high-profile and complex mergers and acquisitions in the telecommunications, mining, financial services, real estate, manufacturing, and technology sectors—many requiring international coordination with law firms around the world. The firm has also acted in a number of difficult and complex disputes and mediations, both in Canada and abroad.

In addition to the traditional areas of legal practice, Blakes is recognized for its innovation and expansion into new areas of business law. The firm was one of the first law firms in the country to develop legal expertise in the technology sector, with major clients now in areas such as life sciences, software and hardware development, e-commerce, the Internet, and domain name registration.

Throughout its history, Blakes has demonstrated an ability to provide value to its clients beyond traditional legal advice. In major transactions and lawsuits, the firm uses a multi-

disciplinary approach, leveraging its cross-country offices and industry-specific lawyer teams to swiftly obtain results for clients.

On discussing Blakes approach to servicing clients, James R. Christie, Blakes Chairman, explains: "The first question we ask new clients is, 'What are your business objectives?' It is critically important for us to focus on the business goals of our clients so that we can provide pragmatic and constructive solutions to their legal issues. If our clients are successful, we will be successful."

INTERNATIONAL INVOLVEMENT

In addition to being a leading adviser to the business community in Canada, Blakes is increasingly involved in the international marketplace.

In 1989, the firm established an office in London to provide a gateway to the European financial and business markets. This office, supported by the resources of the firm in Canada, has been involved in a broad array of matters, ranging from the development of natural resources in Russia to advising on the Canadian aspects of a number of recent inter-

national mergers and acquisitions.

A second international office was established by Blakes in Beijing in 1999. Staffed by lawyers with both Canadian and Chinese experience, the Beijing office has already assisted a number of Canadian and international businesses with the establishment of manufacturing, technology, and pharmaceutical joint ventures in China.

Beyond London and Beijing, Blakes lawyers are regularly providing advice and undertaking projects for clients throughout North and South America, Europe, Asia, and the Middle East.

Through its membership in international legal referral networks like Lex Mundi and TechLaw, Blakes also has non-exclusive associations with major law firms in every industrialized nation and most developing countries. This allows the firm to offer prompt, effective, and seamless service where it does not have its own offices. For clients, this means truly global service.

THE BEST AND THE BRIGHTEST

In order to maintain its reputation as a pre-eminent business law firm, Blakes spends a great deal of time and effort attracting, training, and retaining the best and the brightest legal minds in Canada. "We are absolutely committed to ensuring that our lawyers have the expertise and experience required by our clients to compete in the global marketplace," Christie explains. "Accordingly, we are devoting significant resources to the development and maintenance of our talent base."

Internally, Blakes has developed substantial training programs for its students and lawyers, including a National Training Week held annually for all new lawyers across the firm. Externally, Blakes has established the "Blakes National Scholarship and Awards Program," under which the firm makes a number of significant scholarships available to law students who have achieved high academic standing in law school, often in the face of financial or other hardship. Worth more than $1 million, this is the largest award program of its kind sponsored by a single law firm, and represents Blakes' long-term commitment to fostering top-quality legal expertise. "Our hope is that these scholarships will help some of Canada's brightest law students complete their legal studies without the burden of significant student debt, and that the distinction of being designated a 'Blakes Scholar' will be recognized as a mark of excellence in the legal and business communities," says Christie. "We firmly believe that the establishment of this Scholarship Program is an investment in the future, both for the firm and for the profession generally."

FOR THE COMMUNITY AND THE ARTS

Beyond the law, Blakes and its lawyers are heavily involved in the community and the arts. The firm has several multi-year commitments to the capital campaigns of a number of hospitals in Canada, and is a regular patron and sponsor of the arts. Blakes lawyers also serve as volunteer board members for numerous hospitals, educational institutions, and charitable foundations and organizations.

With industry-focused teams, in-depth expertise in virtually every area of business law, and significant involvement in the communities in which it operates, Blake, Cassels & Graydon LLP is a proud and respected member of the legal and business communities. In Toronto, across Canada, and internationally, Blakes means business. 🍁

To address the needs of its diverse client base, Blakes uses a multi-disciplinary team approach. Industry-specific groups of lawyers that draw expertise from each of the firm's six offices are committed to understanding the unique operations of each client's business.

LOCATED IN ONE OF TORONTO'S MOST VIBRANT DOWNTOWN COMMUNI-ities, The Riverdale Hospital is one of Canada's leading—and largest—chronic (complex continuing) care and rehabilitation hospitals. Riverdale's care programs focus on maximizing the potential and health of a varied composite of patients with complex medical

and health needs. For example, such patients might include an individual recovering from joint replacement therapy, a young adult living with physical and cognitive impairments after an accident, or an older patient needing dialysis treatment to counter the impact of advanced diabetes.

Riverdale is situated next to the city's piquant East Chinatown and the beautiful Riverdale Park, which is renowned for offering the best view of Toronto—especially at night when the downtown office towers are silhouetted in the skyline. The picturesque locale was first the setting, in 1796, for the homestead of John Scadding, secretary to Lord Simcoe, and his family. The City of Toronto purchased the land in the mid-19th century to construct the House of Refuge, intended to care for "homeless and helpless persons," by the century's close. The house had been transformed to become Toronto's centre for communicable disease.

In response to epidemics, while the hospital has undergone many renovations and expansions since

its origin in 1860, its mission has always focussed to provide care for people with complex medical needs.

At The Riverdale Hospital's 140th anniversary in 2000, Toronto Mayor Mel Lastman said the facility "has always been a jewel among hospitals for the expert, compassionate care it offers sick and vulnerable people."

INNOVATIONS IN COMPLEX CONTINUING CARE

Fully accredited, The Riverdale Hospital today cares for more than 600 patients daily, ranging in age from 20 to more than 100 years. Reflecting Toronto's rich social diversity, patients and staff represent more than 30 cultures. Through its caring for the whole person—body, mind, and spirit—with grace, dignity, and independence, Riverdale is recognized as a leader in specialized, complex continuing care. The hospital's core programs of continuing care, neurological care, and special needs care consist of multidisciplinary teams that include physicians, nurses, social workers, chaplains, rehabilitation specialists, and volunteers who collab-

orate to provide patients with individualized care.

Former patient, and now Hospital Board member, Arthur Laprés relays the benefits of this tailored approach: "Recovery is a bumpy road that requires many helping hands and loving attention. They [Riverdale] recognize this, and all the achievements along the way."

Riverdale has always been a ground breaker in care, tackling infectious diseases throughout its history, being the first chronic care facility in Ontario to care for HIV/AIDS patients, and establishing a community-based home care rehabilitation agency. Innovative programs have been developed at the hospital to address specialized needs. Riverdale co-initiated Toronto's, and southern Ontario's, only end-stage renal dialysis program. The Riverdale Augmentative Communication Service (TRACS) helps the communication needs of individuals with severe speech and/or physical impairments. Addressing how to deliver the best practices to a multiethnic patient population, the Cultural Interpreter

Situated in one of Toronto's most distinct and diverse urban neighborhoods, The Riverdale Hospital interacts and celebrates with its community. The hospital annually hosts a community festival and sponsors the Dragon Fest held in East Chinatown.

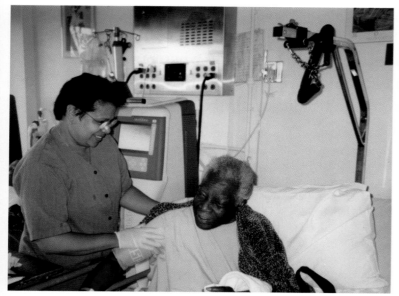

The Chronic Care Dialysis Unit, operated in partnership with Scarborough General Hospital, is among the Hospital's unique programs. Providing both haemodialysis and peritoneal dialysis, the unit serves to better the quality of life of individuals affected by end stage renal disease (left).

Riverdale's rehabilitation programs engage patients, who range in age and condition, in a diverse array of therapies and related activities—occupational therapy, physiotherapy, speech-language pathology, acupuncture, sensory stimulation, hydrotherapy, and aromatherapy— to maximize potential (right).

"The Village on the Park" is envisioned as The Riverdale Hospital's future: A fully integrated health care organization, that is recognized as a Centre of Excellence in rehabilitation and complex continuing care (below).

Program provides patients and families the option to communicate in their first language with staff. The hospital also operates an active Day Treatment Program, as well as a variety of outpatient services, to reduce the impact of chronic disease and to manage the regaining of independence.

BUILDING HEALTHY COMMUNITIES

Riverdale's involvement in the community—geographically and as a health care provider—is readily apparent. Every summer the hospital, area residents, and community groups enthusiastically organize and host the Riverdale Hospital Community Festival in Riverdale Park. Riverdale also supported East Chinatown's first annual Dragon Fest community celebration of dance, music, and food. During the winter holiday season, Riverdale invites the community to light up the largest evergreen in Riverdale Park, along with patients and families, at the Tree of Lights Ceremony.

The hospital also collaborates with a variety of health care organizations to create relationships that improve care and add to programs. Riverdale works closely with local community centres and the nearby acute care hospitals, Toronto East General and The Scarborough Hospital, to provide seamless care. The hospital has established relationships with specialized organizations including the Acquired Brain Injury Network, Multiple Sclerosis Society, Alzheimer's Association, Heart and Stroke Foundation, and Palliative

Care Council of Toronto. Annually, Riverdale hosts the Strangway Clinical Day to examine the future of geriatrics and the Healthy Connections Conference, which invites health care and social service organizations focussed on improving service to southeast Toronto.

RIVERDALE'S FUTURE

An estimated 50 percent of Canadians will suffer from a chronic illness during their lifetime, and Riverdale's commitment to innovation is enabling the hospital to be there to help in as many ways possible.

The hospital's future plans to meet these different needs are extensive. The Riverdale Hospital is expanding and advancing its programs and services to become a Centre of Excellence in rehabilitation and complex continuing care. This future hospital community, envisioned as "The Village on the Park," will offer and integrate a complete range of services from complex continuing care and rehabilitation to long-term and community care.

To realize its vision, Riverdale will bring organizations and people together to provide care and engage in research, education, health promotion, and service to meet the needs of the community. Plans include offering supportive housing and assisted living quarters; developing a research centre; expanding community partnerships; extending services into the community; and constructing much-needed long-term-care beds. For more than 140 years, The Riverdale Hospital has cared for people in the community, and

"The Village on the Park" builds on this great legacy, and a new image launched in fall 2001 reflects the next chapter in the hospital's exceptional history. 🍁

SUN LIFE FINANCIAL

HE SUN LIFE FINANCIAL GROUP OF COMPANIES, HEADQUARTERED IN Toronto, is a leading international financial services organization. Sun Life traces its roots back to 1871, when Sun Life Assurance Company of Canada commenced business in Montreal. From modest beginnings in a small building on Notre Dame Street in that

city, the company grew to the point where larger, more functional quarters were needed—hence the construction of the firm's majestic head office building in downtown Montreal. After its completion in 1933 and through the decades since, the edifice has stood as a proud national landmark and the symbol of solid respectability and prestige.

In 1978, the organization established its headquarters in Toronto. Today, Sun Life Financial once again commands a landmark presence— this time in a gleaming glass tower at the corner of King Street West and University Avenue in the heart of Toronto's vibrant financial district. From these corporate and executive headquarters, Sun Life Financial manages a global network of offices, business units, affiliates, and strategic partnerships in Canada, the United States, the United Kingdom, Hong Kong, the Philippines, Japan, Indonesia, India, and Bermuda.

The lobby of the Sun Life Financial Tower has become more than simply the ground floor of an office building; it has been developed into a showplace for the corporate culture of Sun Life Financial. Entering a spacious and elegant atrium, visitors are welcome to stop at the Corporate Centre—a unique museum-cum-conference facility where they can browse displays depicting the more than 130-year history of the organization and view informative audiovisual presentations. The Corporate Centre also provides a warm venue for out-of-office meetings or small social receptions.

THE CANADIAN OPERATION

Toronto is also home to the head office of Sun Life Financial's Canadian Operations, the hub for all of the company's Canadian business activities. Sales, marketing, communications, product development, human resources, administration, real estate, and finance are all part of this division. In addition to individual life insurance business, this

operations unit handles all corporate group pension, group retirement savings plans (RSP), and health insurance business, as well as group benefit packages, for a long list of large Canadian organizations.

Two of Sun Life Financial's most successful brokerage operations are also centred in Toronto. Spectrum Investment Management Limited is a mass-market mutual fund company whose products are sold by Sun Life Financial agents and are offered through independent dealers and brokers. McLean Budden Limited, with its own portfolio of mutual funds, complements Sun Life Financial's other Canadian operations with its strengths in institutional and high-net-worth individual markets.

In March 2000, Sun Life Financial Services of Canada Inc., the parent

company of the Sun Life Financial organization, appeared on stock exchanges around the world, moving the firm into a new era and marking the end of a complicated demutualization process. Today, from its Toronto base, Sun Life Financial has joined with major international financial institutions to become a world-class provider of financial products and services, and has become that rare business entity—a global enterprise headquartered in Canada.

COMMUNITY PARTNERSHIP

Through its programs of corporate sponsorship, Sun Life Financial is also extremely active in communities all across Canada, and particularly in its hometown of Toronto. Sun Life Financial sponsors a wide variety of worthy programs, ranging from

The Sun Life Financial tower, at the corner of King Street West and University Avenue at the heart of Toronto's financial district (left)

The Sun Life Assurance Company of Canada building in downtown Montreal was completed in 1933 (right).

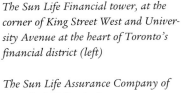

The entrance to the lobby atrium of the Sun Life Financial tower; the Corporate Centre is located to the left

supporting arts programs and youth initiatives to assisting agencies and community groups that are dedicated to improving the lives of residents in Toronto and across Canada.

Programs sponsored by Sun Life Financial include funding for the Heart and Stroke Foundation to enable the purchase of a lifesaving, automated, external defibrillator device, used by emergency response personnel to stabilize heart attack victims. Other funding includes grants to Big Sisters of Toronto and the Toronto Humane Society Animal Rescue Program, as well as a $500,000 donation for research at the Hospital for Sick Children. In 2000, Sun Life Financial also donated $1 million to the University of Toronto to fund the Sun Life Financial Chair in Bioethics.

Whether in business practices, strategic sponsorships, corporate donations, or any of a host of activities undertaken from its Toronto headquarters, Sun Life Financial adheres to its vision of providing excellence and innovation in its products, outstanding service to its clients, better value for its shareholders, and a culture of integrity in all its business dealings. These were the tenets that shaped the firm's beginnings as a life insurance company, and they hold today as Sun Life Financial moves forward into the future as a major international financial services enterprise.

The Sun Life Financial museum, located in the Corporate Centre, depicts the 130-year history of the organization.

THE TORONTO STAR

HE HISTORY OF *THE TORONTO STAR*, CANADA'S LARGEST DAILY newspaper, is one of beliefs, strengths, and forward thinking. On Thursday, November 3, 1892, the first issue of *The Evening Star*, forerunner to *The Toronto Star*, was sold on the streets of Toronto for one cent. The newspaper was a modest four-page edition and

called itself A Paper for the People.

The new paper was started by a group of 25 printers who had been locked out in a labour dispute at *The Evening News*. The first paper was produced on the third floor of The World building at 83 Yonge Street. Six weeks later, the offices were moved to a new home at 114 Yonge Street, where it stayed for four years.

Even during the early years, *The Star* attacked unfair labour practices, supported a minimum rate of wage law, advocated a national form of hospital insurance, and pressed for an independent Canada. But the paper continued to struggle financially, and the ownership changed several times over the first few years. In 1896, new owners moved *The Evening Star* to the Saturday Night building at 26-28 Adelaide Street West.

J.E. Atkinson took over the job of running The Toronto Star *in 1899 and built it up to the biggest in the city.*

THE EVENING STAR

In 1899, a group of leading Toronto citizens bought *The Evening Star* for $32,000. The job of running the paper was offered to Joseph E. Atkinson, who, at 34, was the managing editor of *The Montreal Herald*. Atkinson accepted the job with the understanding that he would run the paper free of influence from the new owners, and that he could purchase stock in the new company. Atkinson was the force behind a period of great growth and revitalization for *The Evening Star*, establishing policies that

aligned corporate objectives with public responsibilities. Those policies continue to guide *The Star* today.

In early 1900, two months after taking charge, Atkinson changed the name of the paper to *The Toronto Daily Star*. In 1905, the paper moved to its first self-contained home with its own presses at 18-20 King Street West. By 1910, circulation had climbed to more than 60,000, which was the largest in the city. During the early 1900s, *The Star* continued to advocate reforms, as it does today, often to the disapproval of both the government and the public. A century ago, *The Star* was urging free TB care, a progressive income tax, unemployment insurance, old age pensions,

racial tolerance, and public ownership of utilities.

By 1920, *The Star*'s daily circulation was close to 175,000. In 1922, the paper became a pioneer in the broadcast field by establishing its own radio station, CFCA. *The Star* continued to grow and prosper and, in 1929, the paper moved to a custom-built, 23-storey building at 80 King Street West. The editorial policy of *The Star* under Atkinson continued to be dedicated to the interests of the man on the street. The newspaper urged the protection of minority rights, labour's rights to organize and strike, and the freedom of the individual from fear, want, and injustice.

Atkinson died in 1948 and his son-in-law, Harry C. Hindmarsh, became president. When Hindmarsh died in 1957, Atkinson's son, Joseph S. Atkinson, was elected president, and subsequently became chairman of the board of Toronto Star Limited. Beland H. Honderich, who had started as a reporter at *The Star* in 1942, became publisher in 1966.

ONE YONGE STREET AND BEYOND

In March 1969, *The Star* announced that it had sold its 80 King Street West property and would build a new headquarters at One Yonge Street. The move took place in 1971. Followin

The Toronto Star *building in 1920 (left), and staff before 1929 (right)*

Honderich's retirement as publisher of *The Star* in 1988, David Jolley, who was also president, became publisher. As the newspaper moved into the 1990s, it became evident that its existing printing presses at Yonge Street did not have the capacity to print the ever-expanding newspaper.

A new, state-of-the-art press facility, the Vaughan Press Centre, was constructed and opened in 1992 on property *The Star* owned near Woodbridge, just northwest of the city of Toronto. Renowned for the superior quality of their colour printing, the presses underwent a $60-million colour extension in 1998 that gave *The Star* more colour capacity than any newspaper in Canada. The giant *Star* presses are capable of printing 48 pages of full colour in a typical 96-page paper.

John A. Honderich, a former reporter, bureau chief, and editor of *The Star*, and son of former publisher Beland Honderich, became publisher of the paper in 1994. Torstar, the paper's parent company, purchased four southern Ontario daily newspapers in 1999—*The Hamilton Spectator*, *The Kitchener-Waterloo Record*, *The Guelph Mercury*, and *The Cambridge Reporter*—to create the Torstar Daily Newspaper Group, which, along with *The Toronto Star*, form the third-largest newspaper publishing group in the country.

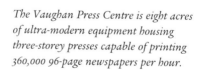

Paper handling at The Star's *Vaughan plant is done by Automatic Guided Vehicles (AGVs).*

A CENTURY OF EXCELLENCE

*T*he *Star*'s tradition of editorial excellence has been honoured with many awards through the years, including more National Newspaper Awards than any newspaper in Canada and the only Pulitzer Prize ever awarded to a Canadian newspaper. In 1998, *The Star* was voted the best media outlet in Canada by the Canadian Journalism Foundation.

Today, *The Toronto Star* has grown from that small paper started by 25 printers into Canada's largest daily newspaper with a staff of close to 2,000 and an average circulation of 455,000 copies, Sunday to Friday, and some 700,000 on Saturday. ✦

The Vaughan Press Centre is eight acres of ultra-modern equipment housing three-storey presses capable of printing 360,000 96-page newspapers per hour.

The Toronto Star Vaughan *plant has a state-of-the-art printing press control room.*

WITH THE OPENING OF ITS FIRST TORONTO BRANCH AT KING AND Bay streets on a cool day in November 1897, Scotiabank began its enduring relationship with Toronto. While the bank originated in the Maritimes, Henry C. McLeod, General Manager, recognized the growing importance of Toronto in the nation's

economy, and moved the general office to the city in 1900.

New branches opened quickly throughout Toronto's neighbourhoods and, by 1919, Torontonians had 21 Scotiabank branches to choose from. Today, there are more than 200 branches in and around the city that are part of a premier international financial institution. Scotiabank is comprised of some 2,000 offices and branches, with more than 52,000 employees in more than 50 countries around the world.

CORE BUSINESSES

Scotiabank consists of four major business areas: Domestic Banking, Wealth Management, Scotia Capital, and International Banking. Domestic Banking provides diverse financial services to individuals and small and medium-sized enterprises in Canada. Customers are served through a national network of some 1,000 branches, approximately 2,000 automated banking machines, and four call centres, as well as telephone and Internet banking. This segment is the heart and soul of the bank, serving about 6 million Canadian households and more than 650,000 small and medium-sized businesses.

Wealth Management incorporates key personal investment and advisory activities that offer clients a comprehensive range of products and services, encompassing mutual funds, full-service and discount brokerage, and private banking and trust. Wealth Management has become an increasingly important part of Scotiabank's business as the baby boom generation focusses on savings and retirement.

Scotia Capital is the bank's global corporate and investment banking arm. The division has recognized strengths in specialized and syndicated lending, corporate debt, mergers and acquisitions, foreign exchange, and derivatives. Scotia Capital's goal is to provide the best financial solutions for the needs of corporate, institutional, and governmental clients.

The first Toronto branch of Scotiabank opened in 1897; the bank's executive offices are now located in the Scotia Plaza tower.

Scotiabank has been a groundbreaking leader in international banking. In fact, before Scotiabank landed in Toronto, it had set sail for Kingston, Jamaica, and opened a branch there in 1889, forming the roots of its Caribbean network. Scotiabank is now the region's leading financial institution, with some 6,000 employees in 20 Caribbean countries.

Scotiabank has long had faith in the growth and potential of countries around the world. The bank now has a strong presence in Argentina, Chile, Costa Rica, El Salvador, Mexico, Peru, and Venezuela, in addition to 11

countries in Asia from Singapore to India. By and large, Scotiabank relies on local management and resources, and offers products and services that reflect the unique customer needs in each country.

With more than a century of international experience, Scotiabank has a solid understanding of how to operate successfully in the global marketplace. Its international reach is one that is respected by Torontonians because, after all, the city is very much an international operation, with people from virtually every nation in the world calling it home.

MEETING CUSTOMERS' NEEDS

Scotiabank is in the business of helping customers improve their financial well-being by providing the right tools for every need and financial goal. Technological advances in banking services have been the great new frontier for Scotiabank. In essence, technology is the newest way in which the bank puts people first.

e-Scotia, Scotiabank's new e-commerce venture, specializes in e-commerce products, sales, service and investments. e-Scotia's role is to invest in the research and development of leading-edge technologies, strategically invest in high-tech companies, and launch new e-commerce products and services to make banking easier for individuals and businesses.

The ScotiaWeb store, developed in partnership with Microsoft, is a one-of-a-kind service used to help businesses become part of the on-line world. Scotiabank's Procuron service provides Canadian businesses with a national, business-to-business exchange to buy business products and services.

But technology is not for businesses alone: *i*:PARTNER is an innovative, single-source, on-line brokerage service that combines on-line research and trading with traditional personal investment advice. Scotiabank's customers can access tremendous resources on-line, and, along with access to regular banking services, Scotia Reality Check questionnaires can help customers plan their financial future.

A COMMITMENT TO TORONTO

Perhaps one of the most important examples of the bank's focus on putting people first is Scotiabank's active commitment to the communities it serves. Scotiabank is involved in every community where its branches are located—from Mexico to India— and the bank is very visibly involved in the city of Toronto.

Events such as the Scotiabank Toronto Half Marathon for breast cancer research and the Leaps and Bounds Walkathon for United Way are great community activities that get employees and Torontonians moving for charity. Scotiabank has been a leader in fighting breast cancer through its ongoing commitment to Mount Sinai Hospital, as well as to other local groups and educational public events.

Scotiabank generously supports important educational and research institutions, such as the University of Toronto. The bank also focusses on very small, local community projects like Eva's Phoenix, a shelter and training centre for homeless youth.

Scotiabank's employees make an extraordinary effort in their communities as well. Recently, the occupants of Scotiabank's downtown offices were asked to participate in the first-ever corporate partnership donation drive for Goodwill Toronto, filling sacks with various non-perishable items.

For more than 100 years, Scotiabank has played a role in making Toronto a great city—and it will continue that tradition of serving customers in Toronto's many communities for generations to come. 🍁

Customers are served through a national network of some 1,000 branches, approximately 2,000 automated banking machines, and four call centres. (left)

Events such as the Scotiabank Toronto Half Marathon for breast cancer research and the Leaps and Bounds Walkathon for United Way are great community activities that get employees and Torontonians moving for charity (right).

Scotiabank has long had faith in the growth and potential of countries around the world and now has a strong presence in Argentina, Chile, Costa Rica, El Salvador, Mexico, Peru, and Venezuela, in addition to 11 countries in Asia from Singapore to India.

THE CANADIAN INSTITUTE OF CHARTERED ACCOUNTANTS (CICA) IS not only Canada's oldest national accountancy institute, but also one of the country's most respected. Having grown from 255 members at its beginning in 1902 to more than 66,000 at the time of its 100th anniversary, the CICA represents a thriving profession

transforming itself through change and innovation. Canada's Chartered Accountants (CA) demonstrate leadership in every area: as the pre-eminent accounting designation, and as expert business advisers in public accounting, industry, government, education, and the not-for-profit sector. A recent national study, *Protecting the Public Interest: The Role of the CA Profession*, showed CAs are the most highly regarded business professionals for ethics and integrity in Canada.

The CICA's mission is to serve the interests of society and the CA profession by providing leadership to uphold the professional integrity, standards, and pre-eminence of Canada's chartered accountants nationally and internationally. With headquarters in Toronto and an office in Montreal, the CICA works with institutes in 10 provinces, two territories, and Bermuda. Canada's premier accountancy magazine, *CAmagazine*, first published by the CICA in 1911, is still going strong.

The CICA and its members take great pride in the CA designation. The rigorous education program, incorporating mandatory hours of work experience in a public accounting firm, includes an exam that is considered to be the most difficult in the industry and is used as a model internationally. Based on nomination by their peers, about 3 percent of Canadian CAs are elected Fellow Chartered Accountants (FCA) by provincial councils to recognize their services to the community and the profession.

Canada's CAs have a strategic focus, an international perspective, and a clear mission: "Our mission is to enhance decision-making and improve organizational performance through financial management, assurance, and other specialized expertise. We act with integrity, objectivity, and a commitment to excellence and the public interest."

STANDARD SETTING

The CICA sets accounting and assurance standards for both the private and the public sectors, and works closely with stakeholders in business, government, and education, as well as with other accountancy institutes around the world, to ensure high-quality standards that keep pace with change. Federal, provincial, territorial, and municipal governments have adopted many of CICA's recommendations, and corporate Canada uses the organization's standards with confidence. Canada's CAs seek to be the leaders in creating, validating, and interpreting information that measures and enhances organizational performance, and to be the obvious choice for financial management, assurance, and other specialized services. To achieve this vision, the CICA's leadership in standard setting

Robert E. Lord, FCA, Chair of the Board of Directors of the Canadian Institute of Chartered Accountants from 2000 to 2002

J. Hyde, FCA, served as the first Chair of the CICA from 1902 to 1904, and served an additional term from 1917 to 1918 (left).

Comparing a century of the CICA's flagship publication: First 1902 edition of The Canadian Chartered Accountant *(right) overlaps a current edition of today's* CAmagazine *delivered to more than 66,000 members (right).*

is of paramount importance. In standard setting, the CICA plays a key role in protecting the public interest in Canada, but the organization's influence and reputation go far beyond the Canadian border.

INTERNATIONAL FOCUS

With the growth of international business and global capital markets, and the increasing acceptance of international accounting and assurance standards by securities regulators, the CICA recognizes that these standards have become a matter of importance for investors worldwide.

The CICA promotes the international harmonization of accounting and assurance standards through its active participation in the International Accounting Standards Board and the International Federation of Accountants, which represents some 2 million accountants worldwide. In addition, the CICA supports the re-

gional development of the accounting profession through its membership in the Confederation of Asian and Pacific Accountants and the Interamerican Accounting Association.

ONGOING INNOVATION

Innovation is a key focus of the CICA. For example, CAs collaborate with other disciplines and business leaders through the Canadian Performance Reporting Initiative to provide innovative performance measurement tools that address the information and reporting needs of the knowledge-based economy. One of these tools is the development of an approach for measuring total value creation (TVC®) for all stakeholders in businesses and other entities. The CICA is also developing a new service called the CA Performance View that CAs can use to help clients better navigate the future of their enterprises.

WebTrust is one of the CICA's best-known e-commerce innovations. Developed in partnership with the American Institute of Certified Public Accountants, the WebTrust seal provides independent, professional assurance to consumers of e-commerce products and services. Available internationally, the WebTrust seal allows firms to cobrand with WebTrust by adding their own names directly below the seal. Also in e-commerce, SysTrust provides assurance to management and customers on the reliability of systems.

CONTRIBUTING TO THE COMMUNITY

Innovation at CICA extends well beyond the accountancy profession. Establishing standards that serve the public interest drives the CICA and its members to be leaders in the community as well. Across Canada, Chartered Accountants are involved in a vast spectrum of not-for-profit organizations, from symphonies to sports and choirs to children's charities.

In its next 100 years, the Canadian Institute of Chartered Accountants will continue to play an important role in setting standards, protecting the public interest, creating new assurance products, and innovating in accountancy education. Chartered Accountants will always be prominent in the international arena, as well as in the business next door. 🍁

Pierre Brunet, OC, FCA, Vice Chair from 2000 to 2002 and Chair of CICA's Board of Directors 2002 to 2004, with some of the Institute's extensive collections of native art from Northern Canada

Tricia O'Malley, FCA, Chair of Canada's Accounting Standards Board from 1999 to 2001, and current member of the International Accounting Standards Board stands by a traditional British Columbia red-cedar totem.

ORKTON SECURITIES INC. IS A LEADING INDEPENDENT INVESTMENT dealer, with more than 650 employees in offices in Toronto, Vancouver, Kelowna, Calgary, Ottawa, Montreal, Halifax, Chicago, and London. The company is one of Canada's most eminent technology investment banks. ✦ Headquartered in Toronto since

1910, Yorkton is a major player in the expanding areas of the new Canadian economy: e-commerce, telecom, biotechnology, and the entertainment sector. The company's success has been recognized in the Brendan Wood International Performance Review, an independent industry study that measures the performance of Canadian investment banks. This review placed Yorkton at the top of the rankings in all aspects of performance in the technology and health care sectors.

"Our clients' success has translated into strong financial results, but our human capital is unsurpassed in Canada," says Scott Paterson, Chair and CEO of Yorkton. "You just have to walk though our offices, and you can feel the energy, the electricity, and the commitment. Our intellectual capital is the envy of every company in the nation."

In 1995, Yorkton anticipated the convergence of science and technology and wanted to be prepared. Yorkton in the early 1990s, with a foundation as a long-standing Canadian investment bank, had become a mining expert. But once it was clear that there would be a paradigm change in business, Yorkton turned its business on a dime. From mining to technology, the company quickly attracted some of the best analysts in the business—people who were passionate, committed, and focussed. The results have been extraordinary.

"The days of international investors thinking of Canada purely as a natural resource allocation in their global equity portfolios are over," says Paterson. "Increasingly, they acknowledge Canadian capital markets as host to a multiple of future technology and biotechnology worldwide category leaders—and Yorkton Securities is right here ready, willing, and prepared," says Patterson.

"Our clients' success has translated into strong financial results, but our human capital is unsurpassed in Canada," says Scott Paterson, Chair and CEO of Yorkton Securities Inc.

PRIVATE CLIENT SERVICES
Yorkton clients benefit from user-friendly, on-line analysts' real-time company research, such as comments on breaking news and changes in recommendations. The company's private client services division includes some 200 professional client advisers culled from the country's most experienced dealers.

Personal attention is critical: Yorkton hosts a number of private client conferences across Canada, spotlighting the company's institutional research analysts and their views on the technology, biotech, and oil and gas sectors. Yorkton's private clients also enjoy daily E-mailed editions of YorktonXpress, offering daily highlights from Canada's public venture capital markets, as well as a brief and easy-to-read summary of the major market movers in Canada and the United States.

EXECUTIVE WEALTH MANAGEMENT GROUP
In 2000, Yorkton established an Executive Wealth Management Group to provide high-net-worth clients with exclusive service, capabilities, and products. Yorkton's clients now have access to a fixed income product desk, U.S. research, a U.S. discretionary managed equity account, client accounts on-line, insurance and estate planning products, preferred interest rates, and higher interest coverage.

In addition, Yorkton's clients have access to new issues from Canada's top technology companies. For example, only at Yorkton could a non-institutional client have participated in the heavily oversubscribed pre-initial-public-offering (IPO) private placements for future NASDAQ IPO hopefuls such as Zero-Knowledge, Electrofuel, or Zenastra Photonics (formerly Nu-Wave).

INSTITUTIONAL BUSINESS
Yorkton's team of 27 investment banking professionals advises and raises capital for many of

Canada's leading private and public technology-based companies. Relationships extend from early-stage private companies to industry leaders. The full range of corporate finance services includes venture capital investing, placements for private companies, IPOs, sales from insiders, and issuer buybacks, as well as fiscal advisory capabilities, strategic mergers, and acquisitions advice.

In the five short years from 1995 to 2000, Yorkton led 118 technology-based financings and raised more than $2.1 billion. The firm participated as lead, colead, or comanager in 242 technology financings raising more than $4.8 billion.

During this time, Yorkton ranked as the number one investment dealer in respect to the number of lead underwritings in the technology, health care/biotech, Internet/e-commerce, and entertainment sectors in Canada.

EQUITY RESEARCH

In the rapidly moving, technology-oriented, new economy, a sophisticated understanding of overall market trends is critical for Yorkton and its investing clients. Yorkton is committed to providing the highest-quality research with a team of 19 analysts covering technology, media and entertainment, lifestyle and leisure, life sciences, and oil and gas.

Yorkton's research group is one of the most comprehensive technology teams in the country. The quantitative and qualitative information provided by the analysts gives clients

the edge they need to make informed judgments and achieve superior returns on their investments. A dedication to research has helped cement Yorkton's position as a leading underwriter of Canadian technology stocks.

PREPARING FOR THE FUTURE

A prerequisite for a leading technology investment expert is a spectacular Web site, so in 2000 Yorkton undertook a radical upgrade of its corporate Web site. The site offers tools for private clients to optimize the management of their personal portfolios, including real-time portfolio analysis, research at

their fingertips, and product details. New clients are welcomed from across Canada—in all centres—to open accounts on-line. Clients are afforded the best of both worlds with the convenience of virtual self-service and the comfort of direct financial adviser involvement.

As to the future, Paterson has a plan: "Photonics, wireless devices, and application service providers will keep the ripple of the Internet big bang expanding for years to come. Meanwhile, the first draft of the mapping of the genetic code was an important step in the future of biotech industry—and Yorkton will be ready for the next wave."

Yorkton's team of 27 investment banking professionals advises and raises capital for many of Canada's leading private and public technology-based companies.

A prerequisite for a leading technology investment expert is a spectacular Web site, so in 2000 Yorkton undertook a radical upgrade of its corporate site.

THE OLD MILL INN

ONE OF TORONTO'S BEST-KNOWN LANDMARKS, THE OLD MILL INN is the city's only boutique meeting and conference resort. Tucked in a picturesque location on the banks of the Humber River, The Old Mill has been a Toronto tradition for special occasions and memorable events for almost 90 years.

The extraordinary advantage of The Old Mill Inn is its location just steps from the Humber Trail.

In 1793, one of the area's first industrial buildings was a sawmill on the banks of the Humber, which provided lumber for the new town of York and eventually Toronto. Several fires, and several mills later, R. Home Smith, a local entrepreneur, opened The Old Mill Tea Garden in 1914 on that site, which quickly became a popular place to enjoy the view of the Humber Valley. By the 1920s, The Old Mill had become a favourite spot to dance to the music of live bands. The Old Mill's popularity inspired several expansions to accommodate the demands for weddings, social events, and eventually meetings and conferences.

Smith wanted to re-create the atmosphere of an English retreat, which is reflected in the company's motto: "In the valley of the Humber, a bit of England far from England." The resort does indeed re-create the country in everything from the dark-wood-covered entryway to the elegant Elizabethan-style furniture and original flagstone floors. The origins of the mill live on, as the original Humber stones of the 1849 mill have been incorporated into the new Old Mill Inn.

UNIQUE LOCATION AND EVENTS

Known far and wide for generations, The Old Mill has created a new history—a people's history of events to remember. The Old Mill is one of the few places where dinner and dancing are available six nights a week. Few locations can compare to The Old Mill for a distinctive wedding, which includes a 16th-century-inspired candlelight chapel. The award-winning gardens provide a spectacular backdrop for photographs.

Banquets and custom catering keep the organization busy year-round on events from intimate, private dinners to major fundraising galas. The Old Mill's peaceful and quiet surroundings are the perfect location for corporate meetings and events, since it combines the convenience of a location on the subway line with the access of the airport just 15 minutes away.

Sundays are family days at The Old Mill, starting with its famous

The Old Mill's peaceful and quiet surroundings are the perfect location for corporate meetings and events.

Sunday brunch and ending with a family dinner buffet; afternoon tea is served daily. Guests are always welcome to browse the facility, along with its antiques and artifacts.

In its 16 distinctly decorated meeting and banquet rooms, the facility can accommodate up to 800 guests. The Old Mill Inn's meeting specialists and wedding consultants can help in planning everything from major conferences to the smallest of family weddings. Attention to detail, quality, service, and value is what makes events at The Old Mill successful, a fact confirmed by a recent independent survey by Goldfarb Consultants. As a result of this survey in 2000, The Old Mill was the proud Gold Award Winner of the Consumer's Choice Award for Banquet and Reception Hall.

A COUNTRY GETAWAY

Since the Kalmar family took over The Old Mill in 1991, with George Kalmar as owner and Michael Kalmar as president, the dream of an Old Mill Inn has become a reality. "Over

the years, there have been numerous requests for overnight lodging, from conference planners, wedding parties, and guests to visitors from all over the globe," says Michael Kalmar. "Finally, we're able to provide exactly what our customers have been asking for and more: a spectacular, one-of-a-kind country getaway in the city."

The stunning new inn, open for business in fall 2001, consists of 60 beautifully appointed, deluxe rooms and suites. The new inn echoes the old-world, English elegance of the conference and event facility with all the modern conveniences. Every room has an all-season fireplace, a high-speed data port, three phones, a 32-inch television, a stereo system, a private bar, and a relaxing whirlpool tub for two. Rooms are located on only one side of the corridor so that each and every room offers a spectacular view of the Humber parkland. In the historic Old Mill building, there are only four suites per floor, so each suite is large, as well as unique.

Indulgence does not end at the door of the room. The inn also boasts

a state-of-the-art spa, which picks up on the richness of the inn's design and The Old Mill's tradition of attention to detail. Spa treatments are custom-designed to calm the frazzled executive or indulge the wedding party. The exceptional quality of this uniquely located spa makes it a very desirable destination for visitors.

The extraordinary advantage of The Old Mill Inn is its location. The Humber Trail, part of the extensive local trail system for walking, biking, and in-line skating, can be found just steps from the inn. Guests can enjoy miles of adventure: woods, meadows, a river, and a lake—a full country escape from the city without leaving the city.

Many memories have been created at The Old Mill, which has been a part of Toronto history for hundreds of years, and entertaining at this location has been a Toronto tradition for some 90 years. "We have a lot of 50th wedding anniversaries," says Michael Kalmar. "It is a proud legacy that lives on in this very modern, English tudor-style facility." 🍁

Clockwise from top left:
Sundays are family days at The Old Mill, starting with its famous Sunday brunch and ending with a family dinner buffet; afternoon tea is served daily.

In its 16 distinctly decorated meeting and banquet rooms, the facility can accommodate up to 800 guests.

The stunning new inn consists of 60 beautifully appointed, deluxe rooms and suites.

Few locations can compare to The Old Mill for a distinctive wedding, which includes a 16th century-inspired candlelight chapel.

NTARIO TEACHERS' PENSION PLAN BOARD OCCUPIES several floors of an office tower at the corner of Yonge Street and Finch Avenue. Although it is located well north of the financial district and the bustle of Bay Street, Teachers' is Canada's largest single pension fund,

building and protecting the retirement income of Ontario's some 150,000 teachers and 80,000 retired teachers.

With assets at some $75 billion and growing, the fund plays an important role in the national economy, providing a source of long-term capital investment for new and established companies in the Greater Toronto Area and throughout Canada. Its investment role has made the pension plan a shareholder in hundreds of companies on behalf of Ontario's teachers and has focussed its attention on responsible investing to ensure that the pension promise is kept.

More than a decade after its 1990 creation, the Ontario Teachers' Pension Plan is doing just that by following its disciplined investment plan and keeping a close eye on emerging business opportunities with the potential to add value to the fund.

1990: INVESTMENT JOURNEY BEGINS

From 1917 until 1990, teachers' pensions were administered by an agency of the Ontario Government. At that time, the fund's $17-billion asset base rested in long-term Ontario government bonds.

All that changed when the Province passed legislation creating the Ontario Teachers' Pension Plan Board—a new, independent organization with a dual mandate: it would continue to look after teach-

ers' pensions, but it would also begin investing the plan's assets in financial markets.

Teachers' newly hired investment managers immediately set about diversifying the fund's asset mix. They used derivatives to rapidly change the plan's asset mix from government bonds to a balanced portfolio, including a large percentage of equities to accelerate the fund's growth.

During the first 10 years of investing, Teachers' posted an average annual return of 13.4 percent, quadrupling the fund's value and turning a $3.5-billion deficit into a healthy surplus. Today, the pension fund invests in many types of assets—everything from stocks to real estate, federal and provincial bonds to private companies, and new ventures in industries ranging from health care and biotechnology to telecommunications and Internet infrastructure.

RESPONSIBLE INVESTORS

Schoolteachers contribute a significant amount of their salaries to the pension plan during their careers and expect to have a financially secure retirement. Although the fund has enjoyed success since 1990, challenges looming in the future emphasize the importance of the investment program to the long-term health of the pension plan.

Approximately 25,000 Ontario teachers have retired over the past few years, leaving two working teachers for every one on pension. That

ratio is expected to fall to 1.5 to 1 in the coming decade as another some 50,000 teachers reach retirement.

The pension board has a duty to be a responsible investor, securing the retirement income of all teachers on their behalf. Responsible investing means making decisions that are in the best interests of teachers. It also means being a diligent shareholder, taking all opportunities to cast shareholder votes to ensure that management decisions benefit owners—the pension plan's beneficiaries.

Teachers' owns 2 to 3 percent of all companies listed on the Toronto Stock Exchange (TSE) 300. Wide company ownership has focussed Teachers' attention on another issue: corporate governance. Good corporate governance occurs when boards of directors properly do their job to protect the interests of shareholders. In order to maximize shareholder value, Teachers' investment managers take corporate governance very seriously—advocating for laws and policies that promote fairness, transparency, and accountability.

While the organization admits there is no guarantee that encouraging better governance will lead to better performance in every company each year, Teachers' firmly believes attention to this matter by large institutional investors benefits all shareholders, either directly, or through their pension plans or mutual funds.

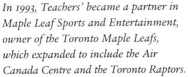

In 1993, Teachers' became a partner in Maple Leaf Sports and Entertainment, owner of the Toronto Maple Leafs, which expanded to include the Air Canada Centre and the Toronto Raptors.

Cadillac Fairview Corporation, the owner-managers of more than 100 prime real estate properties in Canada, including the Toronto Eaton Centre and the Toronto-Dominion Centre (TD Centre) in the downtown financial district. As Teachers' independent real estate arm, Cadillac Fairview is a $10-billion enterprise rivalled by few property companies in the world.

Teachers' trading room, located at its north Toronto office, is linked to markets in downtown Toronto and worldwide.

Teachers' $75-billion investment program has one goal: to secure the retirement income of Ontario's some 150,000 teachers and 80,000 retired teachers.

PARTNER TO CANADIAN BUSINESS

Teachers' tends to keep a low profile about most of its investments. However, a fund of this size has an undeniable impact on the Canadian and Ontario economies. Ownership in hundreds of public Canadian companies is one way the fund is involved. Ownership in private companies through its merchant banking and real estate firms is another.

Teachers' merchant banking activities account for almost $4 billion worldwide, including more than $1.5 billion in Canada, and represent one of Canada's largest active pools assisting companies to fulfill their growth objectives. "We look for companies that have great potential to grow," says Claude Lamoureux, President and CEO. "All they need is investment to expand and move to the next level."

Investment in private companies has made Teachers' a behind-the-scenes partner in a number of Canadian business success stories. For example, Teachers' Merchant Banking Group invested several million dollars in MetroNet Com-

munications in 1996. Three years later, this successful company became part of AT&T Canada, which now trades on the TSE.

WestJet Airlines is another success story. Teachers' was one of the original investors in 1996 when the privately owned start-up company entered the competitive commercial airline industry. When WestJet held a successful initial public offering (IPO) in 1999, Teachers' remained a 20 percent partner in the business.

Teachers' also has a Venture Capital Group that looks for investment opportunities in emerging companies in the health care, biotechnology, telecommunications, and Internet infrastructure sectors. Several of the promising companies in the growing $300-million portfolio have, in turn, been bought by larger high-tech companies looking for sophisticated products that are ready for market. Several other firms have held IPOs subsequent to capital investments made by Teachers' Merchant Banking and Venture Capital groups.

Finally, an important part of any pension plan's asset mix is real estate. In March 2000, Teachers' bought the

PROMISE TO TEACHERS

Ontario Teachers' Pension Plan Board's commitment to teachers is clear and unchanging: outstanding service today, retirement security tomorrow. Since its formation, the entire organization has tried to be the best at what it does. Whether that means finding new methods to add value to the fund or providing fast, personalized service when teachers need it, everything the company does is done for one reason: to ensure that teachers receive the pensions they have been promised.🍁

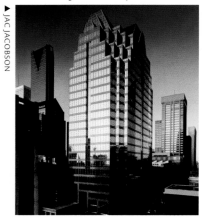

Through its real estate arm, Cadillac Fairview, Ontario Teachers' Pension Plan Board invests in prime retail and office properties such as 1 Queen Street East in downtown Toronto.

▲ JAC JACOBSON

THE CADILLAC FAIRVIEW CORPORATION LIMITED

SINCE ITS INCEPTION IN 1975, THE CADILLAC FAIRVIEW CORPORATION Limited has reshaped and re-invented itself, making it one of Canada's great business stories. After more than a quarter-century, Cadillac Fairview owns one of North America's finest portfolios— valued at more than $11 billion—of retail and office properties.

The Cadillac Fairview Corporation Limited owns one of North America's finest portfolios of retail and office properties.

Headquartered in Toronto, Cadillac Fairview's goal is clear: to enhance the quality, size, and dominance of its portfolio while delivering exceptional cusomer service and financial performance.

A real estate leader with properties in key North American markets, Cadillac Fairview owns or manages 50 percent of Canada's top regional shopping centres; the most productive superregional shopping centre in four of Canada's largest cities; and the number one regional shopping centre in seven of Canada's largest provinces. The company also owns the highest market share of Class A office space in both Toronto and Vancouver.

In March 2000, Cadillac Fairview became a privately held company, a wholly owned subsidiary of the Ontario Teachers' Pension Plan Board. Based on its long-term relationship with Cadillac Fairview, the Ontario Teachers' Pension Plan Board saw the purchase of Cadillac Fairview as an opportunity to expand its holdings in the real estate sector and make a solid, long-term investment. The relationship also works well for Cadillac Fairview, giving the company the opportunity to develop long-term, value-based investment decisions.

TORONTO LANDMARKS

Cadillac Fairview's buildings are frequently the crown jewels of the cities in which they are located, and Toronto is a prime example, with buildings that are truly icons and landmarks—favourite buildings of tourists and locals alike. Probably the most famous of these is the Toronto Eaton Centre, a ground-breaking urban glass atrium shopping mall that boasts four stories of retail space, three office towers, and more than 300 retailers. Each week, more than 1 million people visit this shopping centre, which is one of Toronto's most popular tourist destinations.

The renowned Toronto-Dominion Centre, another of Cadillac Fairview's buildings, is one of the most strik-

The Toronto Eaton Centre is a ground-breaking urban glass atrium shopping mall that boasts four stories of retail space, three office towers, and more than 300 retailers.

ing components of the Toronto sky-line. The Toronto-Dominion Centre, Toronto's very first skyscraper, is widely recognized as Canada's most prominent business address. Designed by the legendary Ludwig Mies van der Rohe and opened in 1967, the centre's sleek black buildings draw students of art and architecture schools from around the globe. The complex not only is singular in its beauty, but also consists of more than 4 million square feet of offices and retail space with 70 stores and two underground food courts. Located at the heart of the financial district, the complex is the hub of Toronto's unique, 11-kilometre underground shopping concourse and walkway.

Portfolio highlights included in Cadillac Fairview's more than 100 properties are Sherway Gardens, Fairview Mall, and Yonge Corporate Centre in Toronto; Pacific Centre and Victoria Eaton Centre in Victoria; Le Carrefour Laval and Fairview Pointe Claire in Montreal; and Washington Square in Portland, Oregon.

FOCUSING ON THE CUSTOMER

An enthusiastic desire to understand and meet the needs of its customers drives the Cadillac Fairview team to create exciting shopping venues and professional, hassle-free office environments.

At Cadillac Fairview, customer service is at the core of creating shopping excellence. Members of the company actively seek regular feedback from more than 6,000 retail tenant customers via ongoing surveys and one-on-one meetings. The company has adopted these measures to ensure understanding of its retail customers' needs, and works to consistently deliver services and programs to help retailers attract shoppers to their stores and prosper in Cadillac Fairview shopping centres.

One example of Cadillac Fairview's measures to promote more enjoyable shopping is *embarq*, a special

The mix of retail businesses in Cadillac Fairview shopping centres reflects the changing needs and habits of shoppers.

lounge for member shoppers at selected Cadillac Fairview shopping centres. This shopper service program provides a clublike, relaxing atmosphere for members, extending the amount of time that customers spend in the retail centre.

High-speed Internet access is yet another Cadillac Fairview service. Recognizing the need for retailers to have cost-effective, broadband connectivity, Cadillac Fairview's tenants can tap into this service at a reasonable cost through a new product called OpteMall.

To create a great shopping experience, it is also important that the mix of retail businesses in Cadillac Fairview shopping centres reflects the changing needs and habits of shoppers. The company prides itself on being expert in reading and predicting shopping behaviour, thanks to intensive market research and decades of experience. Each of Cadillac

Fairview's shopping centres responds to the shopping needs of the community in which it is situated via customized retail mixes.

And while a shopping centre is a place to conduct retail business, retail itself is fluid and always changing. Shoppers' needs change, so retailers facilitate that change; in turn, Cadillac Fairview responds by continually participating in the re-invention of the retail environment. Upgrading and renovation is, of course, constant. Continual innovation is a key characteristic of the Cadillac Fairview approach to retail.

RENOWNED OFFICE BUILDINGS

To ensure that the company's office buildings are the ultimate choice for businesses in Canada, Cadillac Fairview annually spends millions to maintain the highest-quality systems and infrastructure.

The same focus on customer service that Cadillac Fairview brings to retail is also brought to office tenants. In Cadillac Fairview's office properties, a Service Declaration is in place that defines the benchmark by which the company is measured. These standards extend beyond delivery of traditional customer service to encompass the training of all outside contractors, ensuring consistent delivery of service—from loading dock to washroom and from leasing agent to concierge.

For today's office towers, full broadband connectivity is essential, and Cadillac Fairview has accommodated the rise of e-businesses in the firm's buildings, as well as continued to upgrade as technology demands advance.

In addition to being technology savvy, office towers must also be user-friendly and enjoyable for tenants. Generally the first with new services for tenants' use, Cadillac Fairview has launched its first-of-its-kind Web-based concierge service—offering theatre, restaurant, limousine, and taxi reservations—in many of the firm's office buildings.

The Cadillac Fairview Corporation Limited will continue to offer top-of-the-line support to retail and office tenants with the depth and breadth of its research, and the company's ongoing acquisition strategy will always focus on the very best properties in prime markets. Cadillac Fairview, now truly a global company, looks ahead to owning and managing some of the world's other real estate crown jewels. 🍁

Continual innovation is a key characteristic of the Cadillac Fairview approach to retail.

▲ © MARK WILSON

1925
1959

1927	LCBO
1928	Bombardier Aerospace
1928	Fogler, Rubinoff LLP
1930	Honeywell
1936	St. John's Rehabilitation Hospital
1937	Wilson Logistics, Inc.
1938	Boeing Toronto Ltd.
1942	W. T. Lynch Foods Limitd
1949	Marsh Canada Limited
1951	Chubb Insurance Company of Canada
1953	S&C Electric Canada Ltd.
1953	Xerox Canada Ltd.
1954	CHUM Limited
1954	Cole, Sherman & Associates Limited
1954	Ziedler Grinnell Partnership / Architects
1957	AGF Management Limited

LCBO

THE LIQUOR CONTROL BOARD OF ONTARIO (LCBO) IS ONE OF THE largest single retailers of beverage alcohol in the world, offering upwards of 5,000 products in some 600 stores in communities across Ontario. The LCBO also buys wines, spirits, and beer from more than 60 countries for Ontario consumers and licensees. In

partnership with the LCBO, established retailers operate 107 agency stores in smaller, more remote communities. LCBO handles more than 80 million customer transactions each year—making it the government enterprise with which Ontario consumers have the most contact. When customers wonder what wine to serve with red snapper or what port goes best with old cheddar, LCBO has the answer.

Founded in 1927, LCBO was created to regulate the production, importation, distribution, and sale of alcoholic beverages in Ontario. For almost 60 years, most LCBO stores were institutional and intimidating. Customers selected from a price board, filled out a form, and then had a clerk pull the order from the back room. From the late 1960s to the late 1980s, new self-serve stores began allowing customers to roam freely among the stock shelves. However, there was little ambience or service.

LCBO's transformation really began in 1987 when it committed

LCBO has always encouraged enjoyment of beverage alcohol in moderation.

itself to creating a new generation of store designs, developing new marketing efforts, enhancing its buying practices, and placing a new emphasis on knowledgeable customer service.

Change has been strategically driven. LCBO developed five-year strategic and capital plans based on solid customer research and applying the best retail practices. Investment in new and upgraded stores has proved very popular with customers, and has contributed to LCBO's overall success. Such improvements have provided a significant and quick return on investment. LCBO transfer dividends to the provincial government have risen dramatically from $585 million in fiscal year 1993 to $850 million in fiscal 2000. A seventh straight record transfer of $875 million is projected in fiscal 2001. LCBO is Ontario's second-largest single source of non-tax revenue after lotteries and gaming. This

revenue helps to support the wide range of social, health care, and infrastructure programs that all Ontario citizens depend on.

LCBO has gone from a staid bureaucracy to a vibrant, award-winning, customer-friendly, leading retailer whose shoppers are frequently delighted at the breadth of products and depth of service offered. In short, LCBO has become the Source for Entertaining Ideas.

EXCEPTIONAL EMPLOYEES

Customers and LCBO management alike agree that employees have made this transition possible. "I am so very proud of what our employees have been able to achieve," says Andrew S. Brandt, Chair and CEO. "Guided by a strong senior management team, led by Executive Vice President and Chief Operating Officer Larry Gee, they converted an outdated, bureaucratic institution to one of the country's most modern

innovative retailers." In every customer survey that LCBO conducts, employees are always very highly rated.

Rising to the challenge of transforming the organization, employees enthusiastically participated in a number of educational programs. LCBO employees take mandatory product knowledge training courses, and many go on to further their education in the field of beverage alcohol. Customer service training has helped improve the kind of service employees provide. Mandatory responsible service training is also a key part of every LCBO employee's working knowledge. This training includes the Strategies for Managing Age and Alcohol Related Troubles (SMAART) program, designed to help employees serve customers responsibly.

As a testament to the efforts of its employees, LCBO has been recognized with more than 80 national and international awards for retail excellence, store design, staff training, social responsibility, marketing, and communications. In 1997, LCBO won the Retail Council of Canada (RCC) Innovative Retailer of the Year Award and the Socially Responsible Retailer of the Year Award in the large store category. It repeated the RCC Innovative Retailer honour in 1998. The Ontario Chamber of Commerce honoured LCBO in 2000 with its Outstanding Business Achievement Award.

"The LCBO's key strength is its people," continues Brandt. "It has succeeded because of their dedication, talent, and willingness to embrace change."

COMMITMENT TO RESPONSIBILITY

While its stores and product selection have changed for the better, LCBO has never abandoned its commitment to serve Ontario customers responsibly. It is an important part of the culture of the LCBO that employees are proud of and the shareholders—the people of Ontario—value highly.

In fiscal 2000, more than one million individuals were checked under LCBO's Challenge and Refusal Program. Of those challenged, nearly 50,000 were refused service for failing to produce valid proof of age or appearing to be intoxicated.

LCBO has an active and engaged partnership with Mothers Against Drunk Driving (Canada), and is very supportive of the Ontario Community Council on Impaired Driving. Together with these organizations and other social responsibility advocates, LCBO has put an emphasis on responsible service by raising awareness through advertising and educating the public.

LCBO has always encouraged enjoyment of beverage alcohol in moderation, and one of the most significant ways to do that has been through food matching. Linking food and LCBO products began in the early 1990s, and has since become a valued resource for customers. LCBO's award-winning *FOOD & DRINK* magazine was designed to help market beverage alcohol products along with food as part of a balanced lifestyle. The result is a widely popular free magazine that is a valued source of entertaining ideas.

COMMUNITY INVOLVEMENT

LCBO takes advantage of the fact that it is one of the largest store networks of any retailer in Ontario to get involved in local communities. LCBO and its customers raise hundreds of thousands of dollars every year through in-store donation boxes and support for special events. For example, during the devastating ice storm in 1998, which hit Quebec and Ontario, the board's Ice Storm Relief Fund raised more than $90,000 in just three weeks for people whose

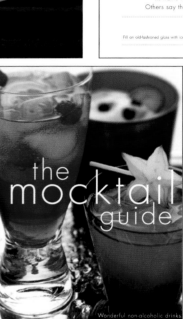

Linking food and LCBO products began in the early 1990s, and has since become a valued resource for customers. The LCBO also offers its customers non-alcoholic drink recipes known as mocktails.

homes and property had been affected.

Every month, two designated charities are the recipients of the funds collected in LCBO's donation boxes. In 2000, the LCBO raised nearly $1 million through its United Way campaign, donation boxes and employee efforts. Past efforts have supported the World Wildlife Federation, as well as athletes participating in the Commonwealth Games. LCBO also supported Toronto's Olympic bid.

The Liquor Control Board of Ontario is fulfilling its mandate by providing excellent service and product selection to its customers; maximizing its dividend to the taxpayers and government of Ontario; and taking a leadership role in promoting socially responsible drinking. LCBO is a valuable—and valued—public asset.

T IS A LITTLE-KNOWN BUT WONDERFUL FACT THAT THE MANUFACTURER of the most glamorous aircraft in the world can be found just a short drive from the heart of Toronto. The city is home to the third-largest civil aerospace company in the world—Bombardier Aerospace and Transportation. ❧ With more than 5,000 employees, Bombardier

Aerospace is the largest manufacturing employer in Toronto. Bombardier's Downsview site was formerly owned by aerospace manufacturer deHavilland, which founded the plant in 1924. Toronto is one of four locations in the Bombardier Aerospace family, which also includes sites in Belfast, Montreal, and Wichita.

Locally, Bombardier owns and operates the Downsview Airport, a former federal government air force base. The airport is now used primarily by Bombardier as an internal corporate flight centre.

Bombardier Aerospace is a unit of Bombardier Inc. Headquartered in Montreal, Quebec, Bombardier Inc. has operations in 12 countries. The company is known the world over for its aerospace technology, rail transportation equipment, recreational products, including the Ski-Doo and the Sea-Doo, and financial and other product-related services.

In its second annual A List, a ranking of the world's premier companies to watch in 21 industries, *Forbes Global* magazine selected Montréal-based Bombardier as the world's leading company in the Aerospace and Defense industry. The *Forbes Global* ranking is based on past performance as well as future earnings and growth potential.

LEGENDARY PRODUCTS AND PARTNERSHIPS

Bombardier Aerospace manufactures a number of critical products at its Toronto site. Perhaps the

most popular is the Q series Dash 8 turboprop airliner family, which includes the 37/39-passenger Q100 and Q200, the 50/56-passenger Q300, and the 70-passenger Q400. These aircraft are renowned for their comfort, efficiency, and economy. The entire Q series is also exceptionally quiet, due to the revolutionary Noise and Vibration Suppression system that isolates passengers from engine noise and vibration. In fact, Tyrolean Airways of Austria calls its Q-series aircraft "The Sounds of Silence."

One of the most interesting aspects of Bombardier Aerospace's work may well be the design and production of the Learjet 45 wing and the final assembly of the Global Express business jet. These customized business jets are sold to movie stars, rock legends, corporate leaders, heads of

state, and royalty around the world.

The Global Express establishes a new standard in corporate aviation, flying faster and farther than any other business aircraft. This aircraft offers a real 14-hour cabin, a cruise speed just below sonic level at Mach 0.85/0.88, as well as the ultra-long range capabilities needed to bring even the most remote destinations closer to home in less time. Eight passengers; four crew members; and considerable office, stateroom, or conference area options can be accommodated on the Global Express. Full or fractional ownership arrangements are available.

The Learjet 45—an eight- to nine-passenger mid-size jet—is the first business aircraft designed and manufactured entirely by computer, thus taking advantage of the precision made possible by the latest technologies.

The Toronto site also helps to control and extinguish fires around the world by producing nacelles for the CL-415, an amphibious multi-role aircraft. In Montreal, the Bombardier Amphibious Aircraft division offers the Integrated Fire Management System, a network of forest protection and fire management professionals.

These incredible airplanes are neither built overnight nor constructed in a single location. Each branch of the Bombardier Aerospace

With more than 5,000 employees, Bombardier Aerospace and Transportation is the largest manufacturing employer in Toronto.

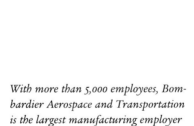

network, as well as manufacturers owned by other companies, contributes its expertise to parts and systems. Partnerships capitalize on the unique experience available at each site, and they also diffuse the cost of new product development. Some of Bombardier's world-leading partners include Mitsubishi Heavy Industries, Honeywell Inc., Pratt & Whitney Canada, and Rolls Royce. Partnerships in this industry are critical, and Bombardier has long been a forerunner in developing these alliances.

DRIVING TORONTO TO WORK

During their 30-year partnership, Bombardier Transportation and the City of Toronto have built a strong bond, working as a close-knit team focused on supplying the city with world-class public transportation. Through Toronto's investment in public transit, Bombardier's transportation facilities in Kingston and Thunder Bay employ thousands of Ontarians.

For decades, Bombardier Transportation has built Toronto's bi-level commuter cars for GO Transit, and the company also provides maintenance and repair for those familiar green and white double-decker trains, which travel to and from the city centre hundreds of times a week.

Toronto's public transit streetcar system is one of the city's most noticeable features. Bombardier, through the former Urban Transportation Development Corporation, supplied the city with its ubiquitous Canadian Light Rail Vehicles. Beneath the metropolis, Bombardier's signature can be found on the Toronto Transit Commission's subway cars, and most notably the latest T1 version. Vaulting across the Scarborough skyline, Bombardier's Rapid Transit light rail cars make the company's presence known.

REACHING OUT TO THE COMMUNITY

The Bombardier site was initially situated far from the hum of the city, but Toronto grew as fast and furiously as a Bombardier jet. Bombardier's manufacturing presence is now a part of Toronto, both symbolically and geographically. Bombardier takes this bond very seriously.

The community of Downsview has grown up near the vast grounds of the plant. Recently, Bombardier began a concerted effort to make a lasting difference in the local community. Bombardier now focusses its corporate citizenship work on investing in Downsview—not simply in terms of local hiring, but also in terms of investing in education, health care, and nearby social service agencies. Programs to date have included high school scholarships, donating computers and Internet time to schools, and implementing the program kids enjoy most—an aerospace curriculum for Grade 6 students.

As a good corporate citizen, Bombardier also concerns itself with protecting the environment for the benefit of present and future generations. Bombardier is committed to taking the necessary measures to mitigate the effects of manufacturing on the environment. This includes the adoption of strict guidelines, standards, and contingency measures aimed at ensuring the safe and ecological management of the company's activities, materials, and wastes.

With its presence in Downsview and its historical and ongoing commitment to public transportation in the city, Bombardier has become—and will continue to be—an integral part of the fabric of Toronto. 🍁

Focused on the Downsview Community and Toronto Charities, Bombardier Aerospace reaches out to the community through corporate donations and community involvement.

During their 30-year partnership, Bombardier Transportation and the City of Toronto have built a strong bond, working as a close-knit team focused on supplying the city with world-class public transportation.

FOGLER, RUBINOFF LLP

 ANADIAN ORGANIZATIONS AND INDIVIDUALS RELY ON THE INtelligent, creative, and personal legal advice provided by Fogler Rubinoff LLP, a mid-sized, full-service law firm with offices in the heart of downtown Toronto. Fogler, Rubinoff counts among its clients numerous individuals, family businesses, professionals

and entrepreneurs, many of whom have been clients of the firm for more than 25 years. Fogler, Rubinoff also represents a variety of financial institutions, securities industry clients, and public corporations, and often acts in complex, high-profile transactions and proceedings.

Fogler, Rubinoff prides itself on providing value-added business, legal advice, and quality service to its clients. Clients have seen the proof of this commitment, and the firm's client list of innovators demonstrates the confidence that clients have in the firm's work. The founders of several major public corporations and other public entities have relied on Fogler, Rubinoff for legal assistance since the inception of their enterprises. These clients are often leading Canadian business visionaries. For the last several years, a client of Fogler, Rubinoff has been honoured with a coveted Entrepreneur of the Year Award, selected from candidates throughout Canada.

DEDICATED TEAMS OF EXPERTS

Fogler, Rubinoff has assembled a team of experienced, talented legal professionals who specialize in various aspects of the law. These areas include business law, securities law, income tax, banking law, securitization, insolvency and restructuring, mergers and acquisitions, e-business, commercial and securities litigation, construction law, real estate law, information technology, succession planning, and employment law.

Specialized groups have been created at Fogler, Rubinoff in response to client needs. The firm's Investment Dealer Advisory Group, for example, acts for both large and boutique investment dealers across Canada. Fogler, Rubinoff's Financial Services Group has helped major financial institutions bring novel products to the Canadian market. Lawyers in the Securities Practice represent issuers and underwriters in often complex public financings.

A gathering of expertise drives the formation of these groups, but it is client relationships that are at the foundation of the firm's philosophy. Lawyers at Fogler, Rubinoff pride themselves on the solid relationships they form with clients, ensuring the personal attention for which the firm is renowned.

TECHNOLOGY AND THE WORLD

To better serve the needs of its growing roster of e-business clients, Fogler, Rubinoff has recently expanded its Information Technology Group. The firm's technology lawyers are experts in this sophisticated and continuously developing area, and

provide superior guidance and innovative solutions to its clients. Coupled with the experience of its business and securities lawyers, Fogler, Rubinoff sees itself partnering for the long term with new-economy entrepreneurs.

Fogler, Rubinoff's membership in the International Lawyers Network gives clients access to some 4,000 of the most skilled legal minds in 59 countries around the world, allowing them to more easily transact legal business around the globe. This affiliation, coupled with the firm's solid foundation and commitment to client service, has positioned Fogler, Rubinoff to best meet the challenges of the 21st century worldwide.

Firm founders Lloyd S. D. Fogler, Q.C. (left) and Melvyn P. Rubinoff, Q.C.

NO MATTER WHO THE CUSTOMERS ARE, WHAT THEY DO, AND WHERE in the world they live, work, or travel, Honeywell technology makes people's lives easier in thousands of ways every day. A Fortune 50 company, Honeywell is a multibillion-dollar, diversified enterprise with more than 120,000 employees

operating in almost 100 countries around the world. With its history in Toronto dating to 1930, Honeywell employs almost 5,000 people in some 50 locations in Canada alone.

Honeywell is famous not only for environmental and process control systems, but also for avionic systems and accessories, aircraft engines equipment and service, hardware products, specialty chemicals, automotive products, electronic materials, and logistics services. The company has an exceptional range of products that really do touch people's lives constantly.

CONTINUAL GROWTH

Honeywell's continual growth around the world has been remarkable. Over the past several years, the company has extended its global reach, with mergers and acquisitions, to include whole new ranges of technology and products. Strategically, this investment in new opportunities has been designed to strengthen the portfolio.

The emphasis on growth has given prominence to the use of Six Sigma quality tools to drive productivity and process improvements. Honeywell is focussed on building a customer-centered culture, and the entire global company is dedicated to meeting customer needs, sharing expertise, and developing solutions for success.

Beyond a corporate culture of delighting its customers, the mantle of Honeywell's success rests on both the technology and innovation in products that customers demand and on the people of Honeywell who make it all happen.

Honeywell's technology and products do well because they are always improving. The organization invests significantly in research and development in order to maintain its status as a global innovator.

Honeywell's Toronto engineers have developed products used around the world. Some of these include oil movements and storage software, which increases efficiency and safety

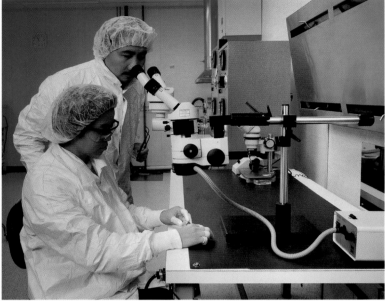

in oil refinery tank farms, and Intelliguard 9000, a specialized security system for the banking industry. Honeywell engines and systems have been breaking ground in aircraft electric power for Dash 8s and NASA. Honeywell's Canadian contingent has had significant impact on the global business.

PEOPLE OF HONEYWELL

Particularly in Canada, Honeywell is extremely proud of the diversity of its staff. People from all corners of the globe work in the company's Toronto-area facilities in Scarborough and Mississauga, where its Canadian headquarters are located. Their backgrounds are often varied, and Honeywell employees think their employer is remarkable: Honeywell has been rated best managed company and best company to work for by national and international business publication surveys.

Both of Honeywell's Toronto-area facilities are ISO 9001 certified, and the Scarborough facility has won the Canadian Business Award of Excellence from the National Quality Institute, as well as being ISO 14001 (environmental standard) certified.

Honeywell's commitment to training and education has made these accolades possible. The company

actively encourages lifelong learning through a number of programs. The company offers college-level courses in partnership with Humber College, and, internally, every employee enjoys the opportunity to participate in new learning programs that focus on improving skills, mastering new technology, or developing new systems and strategies.

Growth, innovation, customer focus, and lifelong learning have all contributed to making Honeywell a great Canadian success story. ♦

Clockwise from top: Honeywell's innovative approach to research and development continues to unlock opportunities for growth in aerospace applications.

Honeywell's service technicians respond to customers' building maintenance and operation needs 24 hours a day.

Honeywell's Canadian headquarters is located in Mississauga, Ontario.

St. John's Rehabilitation Hospital

ERVING RESIDENTS OF THE GREATER TORONTO AREA AND ACROSS the province, St. John's Rehabilitation Hospital is one of Canada's leading specialty rehabilitation teaching hospitals. This dynamic and innovative organization specializes in the rehabilitation of adults with the most complex of needs, including traumatic injuries

amputations; cardiovascular surgery; reconstructive surgery; and neurological, medical, and surgical conditions. With its 185 inpatient beds, combined with Ambulatory Care, Marketed Services, and Outreach Services, St. John's Rehabilitation Hospital handles more than 19,500 patient visits a year. The hospital's scope encompasses outstanding program delivery, teaching, and research activities. St. John's Rehabilitation Hospital's dedication to the pursuit of excellence in these three areas makes it expert in the field of specialty rehabilitation.

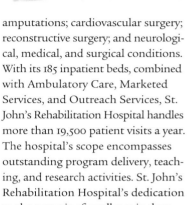

Exemplary Programs

The goal of the hospital's rehabilitation programs is simple: to empower patients to resume active and productive lives. The hospital is dedicated to maximizing its patients' independence and quality of life in their return to the community, while respecting the dignity and uniqueness of each individual.

To achieve this result, all of the hospital's inpatient and outpatient rehabilitation programs are aligned as distinct areas of specialization, with the full range of rehabilitation professionals and medical special-

St. John's Rehabilitation Hospital's Agnew Wing

Working with patients and their families helps maximize functional independence (left).

St. John's Rehabilitation Hospital's goal is to empower patients to resume active, productive lives (right).

ists to ensure a seamless continuum of services.

Core programs include Amputee, Trauma, Burn, Oncology, Cardiac, Organ Transplant, and Neurological Rehabilitation (including complex stroke and neurodegenerative diseases), as well as the Complex Musculoskeletal and Rheumatological Disorders Program. Each year the hospital continues to enhance its programs to accommodate the ever

increasing complexity found in its patient population.

For example, the hospital was very proud to launch Canada's first dedicated six-bed rehabilitation burn program. This unique program, the first to be funded by a provincial health ministry, is enabling the hospital to become a national centre of excellence for burn rehabilitation care, research, and teaching.

St. John's Rehabilitation Hospital is very active in the area of disease prevention and health promotion. St John's Rehabilitation Hospital commonly deals with patients who may have experienced an accident involving complex trauma, including severe burns, or who may be suffering from certain disease conditions such as stroke, multiple sclerosis, arthritis, and diabetes. As part of its community outreach program, the hospital operates public forums to meet the education support needs of the community.

The hospital operates the Back on Track Program, which provides rehabilitation care to individuals injured in a motor vehicle accident. These complex injuries require highly specialized treatment, which is provided by a tightly knit team of occupational therapists, physical therapists, massage therapists, nurses, speech language pathologists, social workers,

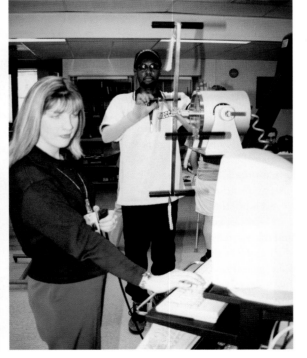

COURTESY OF THE NANCY E. REID COLLECTION

psychologists, and physicians.

St. John's Rehabilitation Hospital is proud to operate as a Specialty Clinic for the Workplace Safety and Insurance Board (WSIB) in Ontario to help workers who have sustained serious injuries such as burns, amputations, and complex trauma. Highly trained teams create personalized treatment plans for each patient, expediting his or her road to recovery and re-entry into the work force. All of these programs involve working with patients and families to help maximize functional independence.

The hospital also offers massage therapy, chiropody services, and a chiropractic clinic in conjunction with the Canadian Memorial Chiropractic College, providing convenient walk-in services to members of the community.

St. John's Rehabilitation Hospital has always been a leader in providing outstanding specialty rehabilitation care. Over the years, the hospital's programs have evolved to meet the ever increasing complexity of its patients' needs. The hospital is driven to increasing the body of knowledge in specialty rehabilitation through its relentless commitment to teaching and research.

COMMITMENT TO EDUCATION AND RESEARCH

St. John's Rehabilitation Hospital is committed to training the next generation of experts in rehabilitation sciences. Through its affiliation with the University of Toronto, St. John's Rehabilitation Hospital has established itself as an academic hospital, thereby supporting its service mandate

through research and teaching to provide evidence-based, highly specialized care. The hospital plays an active role in the training of medical and rehabilitation science professionals from across Canada and around the world.

St. John's Rehabilitation Hospital has actively been engaged in research initiatives with several acute care hospitals and other rehabilitation hospitals, as well as the WSIB. The hospital is making important strides in creating a major research enterprise focussed on its unique rehabilitation specialties. Academic and other health sector partnerships are helping the hospital stay on the cutting edge of innovation in this area.

HISTORY

Founded in 1936 by the Sisterhood of St. John the Divine, St. John's Rehabilitation Hospital's location is truly spectacular: rolling hills, green lawns, and blooming flower beds against the background of a lush forest. With 31 beautifully treed acres in the northern part of Toronto, the hospital has a uniquely peaceful and idyllic setting, making it a perfect place for focussed, specialty rehabilitation. From the beginning, the Sisters ensured that St. John's Rehabilitation Hospital was grounded in spiritual values and that care was provided using a holistic approach.

Prior to the founding of the hospital, the Sisterhood ran a school of nursing, and had a long history of providing convalescent and rehabilitation care. Sister Beatrice, the first administrator of St. John's Rehabilitation Hospital, said in 1938 that "the recovering patient must

be set in an environment that will send him back to his life and citizenship vigorous and wholesome in body, mind, and spirit." This commitment to helping people back to their lives continues today at St. John's Rehabilitation Hospital.

THE FUTURE

Pursuing excellence is an ongoing process in which no organization can afford to stand still. Therefore, it is expected that St. John's Rehabilitation Hospital will continue to pursue its mission of providing outstanding specialized rehabilitation throughout the continuum of care. This will be achieved by continuous innovation in patient care. Furthermore, patients and their families can expect a strong emphasis on research and education, as well as on community-based services that meet the evolving needs of patients and clients. This is the foundation the hospital will be building on as it grows, modernizes, and expands its facilities. 🍁

The Ashforth Memorial Garden is one of many special places to visit on St. John's Rehabilitation Hospital's 31 beautifully treed acres (left).

Sunrise highlights St. John's Rehabilitation Hospital's scenic walkways and grounds (right).

Individually customized rehabilitation is one of the hallmarks of care at St. John's Rehabilitation Hospital.

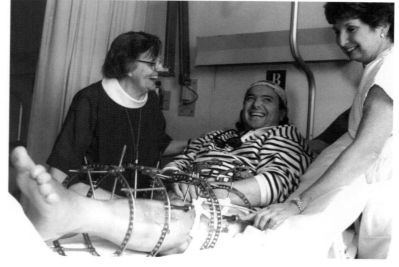

WILSON LOGISTICS, INC.

HE SIGNATURE RED OF A WILSON TRUCK HAS BEEN A FAMILIAR SIGHT IN the Toronto area for more than half a century. Founded in 1937, Wilson Transport has long been a part of the Toronto and Ontario transportation industry. Current Chairman and CEO James Wilson represents the third generation in this successful family-run business.

A TRANSPORTATION LEGEND

Chances are, if you eat in Ontario, your food has been delivered by Wilson. Wilson Logistics, Inc. transports more than 48 percent of the food in the entire province. Wilson has come a considerable distance from its first incarnation, Wilson Transport Corporation. The father-and-son team of John and Carl Wilson saw an emerging market in efficient food transportation from the vantage point of their farm near the Holland Marsh, just north of Toronto. The Wilsons' farm truck became a delivery vehicle for local growers, and soon after that they bartered the farm away entirely in exchange for four tractor trailers.

Due to their connections and expertise in the farm community, the Wilsons focussed on food delivery and cultivated strong and long-lasting relationships in the grocery industry. The company counts among its major customers some of the biggest names in the Canadian grocery industry at the time, including A&P, Dominion Stores, and Sobey Foods.

The Wilsons quickly became pioneers in Canadian food transportation, developing systems and logistics methods long before those terms came into being. In 1950, Wilson Transport operated the first tractor-trailer shipment west of Sudbury in northern Ontario. Prior to this innovation, the only way to transport products and produce into Sault Sainte Marie, located 700 kilometres northwest of Toronto, was by train.

Wilson's Truck Lines Limited established itself in Etobicoke—in western Toronto—in 1967 due primarily to the proximity of Canada's largest grocery distribution support centers. The location has continued to be an excellent choice, situated relatively close to downtown and only a stone's throw from the city's major highways.

The foundation of the Wilsons' business has always been as food carrier specialists—its bread and butter—providing heated and refrigerated transport services across North America. But extensive experience in the market drew the firm to logistics and solutions consulting. "The grocery business, with its slim profit margins, taught us some tough lessons about maximizing efficiencies," says James Wilson. "So we can now pass that learning on to our customers."

In 1998, Wilson recognized the need for a Canadian logistics company that could meet all the needs of local industry. Wilson Logistics, Inc. was formed to offer all components of transportation—a full menu of services that include trailer leasing, truck leasing, and comprehensive logistics consulting. Wilson's services can also be invisible on the road: Logistics modelling and private fleet management, for example, are custom tailored to each client. In fact, the Wilson Logistics group is comprised of five individual, but linked, corporations: Wilson Logistics, a lead logistics provider; Specialized Motor Express, an international motor carrier; Trailcon Leasing, a Canadian trailer and intermodal specialist; Wil-Truck Leasing, a dedicated truck leasing company; and Wilson's Truck Lines, a dedicated food motor carrier.

"We can help anyone requiring transportation," says Wilson. "'Never say no' is our service policy."

The company's extensive menu of services includes logistics modelling, dedicated logistics, dashboard logistics, trailer leasing, truck leasing, for-hire carrier, and personnel services. Customers can choose exactly what services—and how much of each service—they need.

As an organization, Wilson focusses on its key strengths: delivering quality

Wilson Logistics, Inc. was formed to offer all components of transportation, a full menu of services that include trailer leasing, truck leasing, and comprehensive logistics consulting.

customer service, state-of-the-art technology, a strong management team, and innovative, practical solutions.

EXCEPTIONAL EXPERTISE

Wilson Logistics boasts an exceptional group of highly skilled professional engineers and accountants, considered scientists in the field of logistics. In the past several years, the company has provided logistical consulting to some of Canada's major retailers. "A proactive approach to improving an organization's distribution supply chain can be tremendously beneficial to business," says Wilson.

Not only does logistics consulting provide a valuable stand-alone service for customers, but also the expertise adds value to all of the other divisions of the organization. For example, dashboard logistics is a tool that marries innovation in technology with very practical transportation needs. With the Wilson dashboard, clients may track all shipping information via the Internet, including such complex needs as reverse logistics.

Wilson customers can also take advantage of full-service truck leasing. Not only can their immediate transportation needs be met, but clients can also have access to logistics data that will help them assess equipment needs for optimal requirement and usage. Wilson engineers can create comprehensive operating models, a service they provide for most clients. These models create individualized and maximum efficiency distribution systems from point of manufacture to point of sale.

FIELD TO FORK— RECYCLING TO LANDFILL

Wilson Logistics expanded its services in 2001 to include the haulage of solid waste. This was a natural fit, completing the transport logistics supply chain. The company has contracts with the City of Toronto and Mississauga, providing solid waste transportation services.

Wilson Logistics prides itself on its ability to offer customized logistics solutions—from the simplest provision of transport or truck leasing to the most complex modelling of a distribution network. Wilson functions as a department within a client organization and is fully accountable for services performed. The combination of Wilson's flexibility and responsibility gives client companies a greater level of security—the company can outsource only what it needs to.

"We have a commitment to our customers," says Wilson. "We won't let them down." ⁂

Wilson has come a considerable distance from its first incarnation, Wilson Transport Corporation. The father-and-son team of John and Carl Wilson saw an emerging market in efficient food transportation from their farm near the Holland Marsh (top left).

Adding the service of hauling solid waste completed the transport logistics supply chain (top right).

The signature red of a Wilson truck has been a familiar sight in the Toronto area for more than half a century (bottom).

THE HISTORICAL HOME OF THE LEGENDARY AVRO ARROW AND THE manufacturer of wings for seven major airplane programs, Boeing Toronto Ltd. is a place where more than 2,800 airplane wing sets have been manufactured. It is an extraordinary story of aviation and triumph. ❧ Boeing Toronto Ltd. is an international wing production site for the Boeing Company, one of the world's leading aerospace companies. While Boeing Toronto Ltd. is an important player in the world-class company that produces products for the global market, the firm has an exceptional reputation in its own right.

RICH HISTORY OF AVIATION

Boeing Toronto Ltd. has been a landmark site in Canadian aviation since 1938, producing renowned airplanes such as Lancasters, Avro Ansons, and the infamous CF-105 Avro Arrow fighter. After the Avro Arrow era, the DeHavilland Company began producing DC-9 wings in Boeing's Toronto facility. Over the course of the facility's illustrious history, successive mergers—involving Douglas Aircraft, McDonnell Aircraft, McDonnell Douglas, and finally the Boeing Company in the late 1990s—strengthened the Boeing landmark.

Boeing's Toronto location is known to Canadians for its role in history, but they would be amazed to see what a remarkably modern, bright, extraordinary expanse of a facility it is inside. A walk through the massive plant quickly reveals that its airplane wings are built to the most exacting standards with meticulous attention to detail.

NEW BUSINESS, NEW PRODUCTS

One of the newest product lines in the Boeing Commercial Aircraft Group is the 717-200, a 106-seat aircraft specifically designed for the emerging regional market. The 717-200 provides full-size jetliner comfort, features low operating costs, and is environmentally friendly. As the supplier of the wings for the 717-200, Boeing Toronto Ltd. is a crucial part of the global team of suppliers manufacturing components for this aircraft.

Boeing Toronto Ltd.'s current aerospace facility takes advantage of its prime location near the airport, rail lines, and major highways, and has expanded its wing production capabilities to become a major spares supplier. The company has developed partnerships with nearly 400 Canadian suppliers, the majority of which are located in the Greater Toronto area and Montreal.

Boeing Toronto Ltd. utilizes a strong on-site programming centre and a state-of-the-art DNC system for quick turnaround of new parts.

Boeing Toronto Ltd.'s current aerospace facility takes advantage of its prime location near the airport, rail lines, and major highways, and has expanded its wing production capabilities to become a major spares supplier.

longer enough to have an expert grasp of your own business. You must also have an excellent understanding of your clients' business, the environment in which they are operating, and how best to respond to their unique needs."

This is particularly true at a time when a growing proportion of business for many companies is now taking place beyond the borders of their home countries. This gives rise to greater risk not only from traditional areas such as property, casualty, marine, and aviation, but also from new and potentially severe exposures related to trade, currency, credit, and political instability that can impede strategies for international growth.

The convergence of insurance and capital markets has brought an explosion of innovation in effectively managing risk, and Marsh has remained at the forefront in the development and utilization of new risk transfer and risk financing solutions. Some examples include insurance that guarantees tax opinions against unfavourable rulings; coverage for the external costs associated with aborted acquisition bids or defending against hostile takeovers and proxy fights; protection against commodity price increases, fluctuations in interest and currency rates, and the effects of weather on sales and costs; insurance that guarantees a company's revenue streams; and products that cap or transfer a variety of liabilities—environmental, securities, or breach of patent or contract—to improve a company's risk profile and consequently add to its value.

Finding the right solutions requires brokers who possess the knowledge and expertise to help clients determine which methods are best in a given circumstance, and then adapt the new techniques to meet their needs.

Marsh's skilled risk management advisers are able to bring all organizational risks—hazard, financial, strategic, and operational—into a total strategy that treats widely varying exposures in terms of their combined impact on the value of the enterprise as a whole.

The company also fulfils the increasing need by clients for advice

CHARLES WESTERMAN

on trends in the marketplace, the health and stability of insurers, the availability of new products and services and how they work, and changing laws in various jurisdictions around the world. These clients rely on Marsh's research and global experience to benchmark how other companies have addressed similar risk management challenges, thus assisting them in choosing the solutions best suited to their needs.

In response to a growing focus by companies on loss prevention in their day-to-day operations, Marsh provides technical expertise and cutting-edge solutions in a wide range of areas, such as process safety management, supply chain analysis, technology threat analysis, environmental risk assessment, and disaster recovery planning.

For the still very important transfer of risk to insurers, Marsh

has developed a global brokering system, using the latest technology to capture valuable market and transaction information and to match clients' risk profiles with insurance placements, enabling the company to arrange the best and most cost-effective coverage. These capabilities provide Marsh with potent medicine for solving clients' problems.

In recent years, the brokerage industry, once considered as dull and predictable as a mill pond, has become a sea of change, and Marsh Canada Limited is determined to remain the most proficient sailor.

"Even when things are running smoothly, when we think we're at the top of our game, we are constantly searching for new ideas and ways to improve what we do," says Rankin. "In today's environment, resting on one's laurels is a luxury we cannot afford."

Marsh provides a broad range of products and services to industries in all segments of the Canadian business community.

S&C Electric Canada Ltd.

ROM THE STREET, THE NEAT BRICK BUILDINGS OF **S&C Electric** Canada Ltd. seem somehow simple, but one step inside the facility reveals a large and sophisticated operation dedicated to the manufacture of products that would be quite unfamiliar to most people. S&C manufactures products that

protect and control medium- and high-voltage electric power circuits. S&C switches, fuses, and enclosures are hundreds of times larger than anything like those used at low voltage. S&C is one of the world's leading specialists in electric power switching and protection.

S&C provides equipment to some of the Toronto area's most famous landmarks, including BCE Place, Pearson International Airport, and the Canadian Broadcasting Corporation (CBC). The company also supplies a broad range of products to Hydro One, Toronto Hydro, and Enersource Hydro Mississauga.

"Electricity must flow continuously and without variation in quality," says John W. Estey, President and CEO of the firm's parent, S&C Electric Company. "People's businesses—and even their lives—depend on it. This is where our products play a crucial role." Specialization has enabled S&C to build exceptional knowledge of application practices and the critical need for reliable products that perform dependably over decades of service. This unique expertise is continually being

updated and utilized to innovate new products and pioneer new applications.

TORONTO BASED WITH A GLOBAL FOCUS

S&C Electric Company was founded in 1911 in Chicago with the invention of an innovative, reliable, high-voltage fuse developed by two men, Edmund O. Schweitzer and Nicholas J. Conrad—hence the

initials S&C. The S&C Liquid Fuse went on to help change the shape of the electric power industry with reliable circuit interruption. By the end of World War II, demand for electricity had increased exponentially—and so, in turn, had the need for more refinements in transmission and distribution. In 1953, Alex Morrison, a sales representative of S&C products in Canada, convinced the founding family to begin manufacturing in Canada, and so, S&C Electric Canada Ltd. was born.

In 1953, the company began in a small, rented facility on Vansco Road in the then Borough of Etobicoke. After only seven years there, S&C purchased 3.9 acres of land on Belfield Road in Etobicoke and built 40,000 square feet of office and manufacturing space. Regular expansions to the property and facility have occurred, with the company currently occupying 230,000 square feet on almost 12 acres of land. The firm is just putting the finishing touches on a 44,000-square-foot addition that will house a new laser cutting centre, increased fabrication space, and significant enhancements to the metal finishing facilities.

S&C Electric Canada Ltd. is a wholly owned subsidiary of S&C Electric Company, but operates like an independent company. S&C

S&C Electric Canada Ltd. was born in 1953 after Alex Morrison (center, with shovel) convinced the founding family of S&C Electric Company in Chicago to begin manufacturing in Canada.

In 1960, S&C purchased 3.9 acres of land on Belfield Road in Etobicoke and built 40,000 square feet of office and manufacturing space.

manufactures a broad range of products, with some manufactured exclusively in Toronto for the world market. The S&C complex in Chicago also manufactures a broad range of products, again with some manufactured exclusively for the world market—an arrangement the company calls "product sharing." Product sharing allows each facility to develop and maintain a very high level of specialization and expertise, while taking advantage of an international marketing organization.

S&C Canada serves the entire country from its Toronto facility, as well as from sales offices in Alberta, Quebec, and the Maritimes. Beyond its Canadian concentration on product development, manufacturing, and service, S&C Canada is responsible for the sales and marketing of all S&C products and services in the Middle East. It has recently opened a sales office in Abu Dhabi.

INVESTING IN EXPERTISE

S&C knows its greatest assets are its people. Estey explains, "We invest in our people and welcome their ideas. That, in essence, is the foundation of our company. We're also innovators and world leaders in what we do. That attracts the best and brightest in the industry."

S&C has always been acutely aware of its obligation to maintain the highest of safety standards in its products. In 1990, the company also initiated an internal safety program aimed at eliminating all lost-time injuries in its operations. "The results of this program have been phenomenal," says Grant Buchanan, President, S&C Canada. In 1996, marking five years without a lost-time injury, S&C was recognized for its safety achievements by the Industrial Accident Prevention Association (IAPA) and by the City of Etobicoke. "We continue to focus on improving our safety program. In 1998, we also introduced a wellness program to help enhance the long-term health and safety of all S&Cers," says Buchanan.

NEWEST IN HIDDEN ENERGY

Because the company is privately owned, the majority of earnings are reinvested in research and development, facilities, and people. "Private

ownership has been a key advantage," says Estey. "It means we've been able to invest for the long term instead of having to produce results from quarter to quarter, as publicly owned companies must do. This is an essential ingredient in the success of our R and D program."

Retained earnings have also allowed S&C to invest heavily in state-of-the-art machining and processing capabilities. Unlike many manufacturing operations, S&C has also maintained a high level of vertical integration. "Controlling most of the processes and parts gives us better control over the quality and delivery of components and products," says Buchanan. "For those parts and processes we don't control, we establish long-term relationships with high-quality suppliers who share our understanding of the need for quality and reliability."

S&C is continually introducing new products and services to the market. This year alone, six new products were introduced. They include a new device for the protection of substation power transformers that will allow utilities to build smaller and less costly substations without sacrificing critical protection, and the expansion of a unique line of power quality products. These power quality products allow critical process facilities–data processing, microchip manufacturing, continu-

ous process industries, and the like—to ride through sags and momentary interruptions, which have, in the past, caused serious production and economic losses.

For the future, S&C Electric Canada Ltd. will continue creating innovative products that focus on the company's specific expertise: electric power switching and protection. 🍁

In 1996, marking five years without a lost-time injury, S&C was recognized for its safety achievements by the Industrial Accident Prevention Association (IAPA)as well as by the City of Etobicoke (top).

S&C employees celebrated in 1996 when the company achieved its ISO 9001 registration (bottom).

Xerox Canada Ltd.

BEHIND THOUSANDS OF DOORS IN TORONTO'S LEADING companies is a secret to success: Xerox Canada Ltd. From desktop colour printers to state-of-the-art production printing and document management solutions and services, Xerox helps the city's businesses run better.

Xerox's presence is not just behind the scenes, however; it has been part of the Toronto community since 1953. The flagship presence and head office is a commanding building on Yonge Street at Finch Avenue in the north end of the city, which is visible from blocks away. Other locations in—and all around—town include Markham, Oakville, Richmond Hill, and downtown. It is the Xerox Research Centre of Canada located in Mississauga, however, that stops traffic. With its ceramic steel façade, the centre looks very much like a spaceship from the ground; and from the air, the building is clearly and most appropriately shaped like a question mark.

The company is a significant local employer with more than 3,000 employees across the Toronto area.

The Xerox team is an unusual one—it is a virtual United Nations of people, just like the city in which it is located. More than 30 ethnic groups are represented in Toronto's Xerox family, and the company has been consistently recognized as a leader in its field.

ADVANTAGEOUS DIVERSITY

Xerox Canada is part of a global corporation that emphasizes diversity and celebrates differences. Senior managers are evaluated on their ability to hire, retain, and promote minorities and women. Diversity is truly a global priority.

"Not only is there a social responsibility today to be as diverse as your community, there are also compelling business reasons," says Cameron Hyde, Xerox Canada's

President. "Our varied backgrounds allow us to think differently as a company. We get great ideas from our employees about how to do things in new ways, and how to reach new constituencies to expand our client base."

Many companies are committed to the communities in which they work, but few rival the level of community involvement of Xerox Canada. In particular, Xerox's commitment to Canada's Aboriginal community is exceptional. In 1994, Xerox founded the Aboriginal Scholarship Program, designed to help eight students achieve their dreams each year. In addition, internal programs, such as the Xerox Community Involvement Program, are intended to encourage volunteerism and social involvement in communities where Xerox Canada's employees live and work. Xerox Canada provides financial assistance directly to non-profit organizations in which employees or their immediate families are involved.

FOCUSED ON SOLUTIONS

Diversity is a theme at Xerox Canada. Not only does the staff reflect the diversity of the city and the country as a whole, but the company's approach to change and flexibility also applies to business services.

"Our customers appreciate that they can buy from us in whatever way they are comfortable," says Hyde. "Some rely on our specialists for solutions-based approaches. Some just want to take advantage of our great retail products. Still others buy on-line, or want virtual on-line demos. We can do it all, in any combination that makes sense for our customers' needs."

Xerox wouldn't be a household name unless it put customer service first. The first question Xerox associates ask is "What do you need to succeed?" The answer ultimately determines the customized solution that the customer requires. For ex-

Xerox Canada Ltd.'s headquarters is located on Yonge Street at the northwest corner of Yonge and Finch Avenue. With its pinkish hue, modern features, and imposing design, the Xerox Tower is a north Toronto landmark.

ample, most customers report that the volume of electronic and paper documents has increased exponentially, but more often than not, managing that information is not their core competency. Xerox helps its customers focus on what they do best by outsourcing the rest.

One of the key advantages Xerox offers its customers is the fact that it is part of a vast, global company with expertise in virtually every industry in almost every company in the world. As well as Mississauga, there are research centres in California, France, New York, and the United Kingdom, working to break barriers and create the next generation of document technology. It is an extraordinary resource.

Xerox has progressed from the long-held stereotype of "the copier company" to an organization that provides a comprehensive lineup of colour and black-and-white printers for the desktop, right up to high-end digital printing and publishing products. Xerox also develops the software that makes these machines tick, allowing users to print variable, one-to-one marketing materials and bind books at speeds as fast as 300 pages per minute—a practice that is revolutionizing the publishing industry. These Xerox products and customized services are part of the company's mandate to constantly strive to ensure that customers work better, faster, and smarter, regardless of size, budget, or industry.

Like its global parent, Xerox Canada has a network of alliances, particularly in the technology sector, which allow the company to develop creative solutions for customers. Collaboration helps to ensure that all components of document management are coherent, integrated, and seamless. The copiers of yesterday have evolved into digital systems that integrate into an organization's technology infrastructure, managing electronic and paper documents with peak efficiency and effectiveness.

"Our aggressive pace of technology and product development will always be based on the needs of our customers," says Hyde. "Xerox will continue to be the perfect choice for every customer, whether they need a desktop printer or a multisite outsourcing partner." ♦

Peter Ku, Manager of Marketing and Strategic Support, proudly displays a brochure for one of Xerox's managed service offerings.

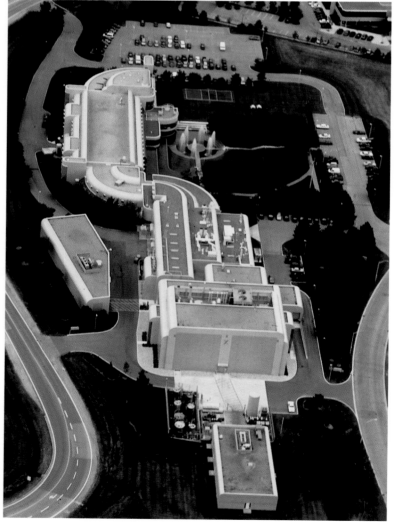

The Xerox Research Centre of Canada in Mississauga stops traffic. With its ceramic steel façade, the centre looks very much like a spaceship from the ground; from the air, the building is clearly and most appropriately shaped like a question mark.

CHUM LIMITED

UST ABOUT ANYONE WHO HAS GROWN UP IN TORONTO CAN RECALL an adolescence spent listening to every fabulous song that 1050 CHUM's legendary DJs put on the turntable. The station's personalities and its perspective on the music scene may have changed over time, but its commitment to growth

and to the city of Toronto remains steadfast.

CHUM Limited operates radio stations from coast to coast; from Halifax to Vancouver, and most markets in between. Content ranging from adult contemporary, talk, sports, and top 40 to classic rock and country has been carefully researched and designed to reach the highest possible audience in each market that CHUM serves. The 27 stations that make up CHUM Group Radio trace their roots back to a landmark building on Yonge Street in downtown Toronto.

Toronto's most famous neon sign shines brightly on the historic CHUM Limited building on Yonge Street.

There's no need to tell a native Torontonian where CHUM's headquarters is located. The building has undergone significant refurbishment to keep pace with the growing media empire, but the address and the much loved 1050 CHUM neon sign have remained the same since 1954.

While its genesis was radio, CHUM Limited, one of the world's largest broadcasting companies, now includes the legendary CITY TV, Cable Pulse 24, MuchMusic, MuchMoreMusic, the New VR, and Bravo—a group of some of Canada's best conventional and specialty television channels. And the list keeps growing.

ROOTED IN ROCK-AND-ROLL

Back in the 1950s, Allan Waters was a young man with ambition who bought a small radio station from his boss. Waters knew that the new music from the South, rock-and-roll, was becoming wildly popular—and Toronto's young people had no radio station devoted to this new craze. Waters stormed into CHUM's original broadcast location on Adelaide Street and simply threw out every record that wasn't on the top 40 charts. Thus, in 1957, CHUM became the first radio station in Canada to play this new format 24 hours a day. Rock-and-roll had found a home.

That same year, 1050 CHUM issued the first CHUM Chart: a list of the top hits of the week. The CHUM Chart came out every week for almost 30 years, and was the first of many publicity efforts that kept listeners coming back for more.

CHUM was the first radio station in Canada to play the hot new foursome from Britain known as the Beatles. CHUM DJs did wild stunts like living in a car and staging an April Fools' day "murder." DJ Mike Cooper even set a world record by riding a Ferris wheel for more than two weeks one hot summer.

Over the years, some of the biggest names in rock-and-roll have visited the station, including Paul McCartney, Donny Osmond, and the Bay City Rollers, who drew crowds of young fans so large that Yonge Street had to be closed.

Waters truly had his finger on the pulse of the city. His particular brand of leadership was an ability to choose the right people. Their compelling personalities would light up the airwaves in the same way that CHUM's television personalities light up the screen today. Jim Waters, Allan's son, Executive Vice President of CHUM Limited and President of

In 1991, Paul McCartney returned to CHUM, the station that first played the Beatles' music in Canada.

ANDREW McNAUGHTAN

CHUM Group Radio, virtually grew up at the station, and has devoted his career to expanding into new radio markets, while maintaining his father's penchant for a people-centered business.

CHUM Is Toronto

The early popularity of CHUM has never faded. Every week, CHUM-FM entertains more than 1 million listeners, and the station has one of the most popular morning shows in the country. The morning trio of Roger, Rick, and Marilyn has dominated morning radio in the city for more than 15 years with informative, witty banter.

CHUM has always been on top of the broadcasting game for a number of reasons: It is a company that is passionate about programming—only the best will do; its mantra is that listeners come first; and it continues to provide the most fun, desirable promotions in the industry.

The future is bright for this company, whose roots in the community run deep. CHUM is ready for digital radio—the L-Band that will bring CD-quality sound, as well as displayable weather, traffic information, and much more. It is the new world of the radio industry in North America, and CHUM will be ready to charge ahead.

CHUM Community

Though CHUM's community involvement over time and across the country is extensive, the company is most proud of one program in particular. This effort, the company's best-known and best-loved charitable event, is the CHUMCity Christmas Wish, a toy drive whereby listeners drop off new toys at the radio stations, the television stations, and the offices of participating sponsors. The toys are in turn handed over to community agencies that distribute them to families in need.

For more than 30 years, Christmas Wish has elicited powerful responses from listeners. It is the biggest toy drive in the country, and the toys consistently fill the halls of the CHUM building to capacity every holiday season. CHUM organizers never fail to be astounded by the generosity of their listeners.

No doubt the most unique aspect of CHUM Limited is its connection to Toronto. The company was, and always will be, a big part of the city, and no other broadcaster comes close. 🍁

Clockwise from top left: Allan Waters (far left), owner of CHUM Limited, joined CHUM staff and performers at a concert promoting Canadian talent in 1959.

104.5 CHUM-FM's Roger, Rick, and Marilyn make up Toronto's favourite morning show.

Charting success: Dick Clark signed CHUM charts for Toronto fans in 1963.

NEIL NEWTON

COLE, SHERMAN & ASSOCIATES LIMITED

THINGS MOVE IN THE CITY OF TORONTO WITH THE HELP OF COLE, Sherman & Associates Limited. In fact, the company, which provides a full range of engineering and architectural services for government and private sector clients, has played a major role in the development of the city's municipal infrastructure—from

expressways to subways, waterways to sewers, and tunnels to bridges. From its office in Thornhill, a suburb on the outskirts of Toronto, the company's some 230-member team of consulting engineers and architects has left an indelible mark on the area's urban landscape.

Founded in 1954, the company has grown from a local business to one that now offers its expertise in transportation, building, and municipal water/waste-water infrastructure to clients around the world. In 1997, Cole, Sherman & Associates Limited became a member of the URS group of companies. URS is one of the industry's largest engineering and architectural firms, with more than 16,000 employees in 38 countries. The partnership not only has brought Cole Sherman international projects, but also has offered clients worldwide cutting-edge technical expertise as a complement to the firm's unparalleled professional services.

LAYING THE FOUNDATION

Cole Sherman made its name in and around Toronto primarily in transportation, municipal engineering, and architecture and building engineering. Cole Sherman has been a leader in these fields since the 1950s. "We've been involved in most of the major transportation developments in the city of Toronto," says Scott Cole, Managing Director and CEO.

Cole is a civil engineer who took over the company leadership following his father's tenure.

Indeed, a survey of Toronto's urban landscape reveals the company's contribution: transportation aspects can be seen in the city's well-travelled highways and essential subway and commuter rail system; in the roadways that traverse the city's multi-ethnic neighborhoods; and the bridges, tunnels, and traffic systems that keep things moving. Municipal water/waste-water engineering is the hidden infrastructure that maintains the city's flow. Municipal infrastructure servicing for the numerous urban developments within the Greater Toronto Area, totalling more than 5,000 acres, is also a major part of Cole Sherman's business. Given the projected population growth within

the Golden Horseshoe, managing efficient designs in this sector is key to providing housing to the economic engine of Canada. Finally, the company's more obvious contributions to the city and its environs are the hundreds of building projects for which Cole Sherman Engineers & Architects Inc. has provided expert advice and professional services.

The level of service the company offers and its close working relationship with the city, local area regions and municipalities, and various provincial ministries are among the qualities that have earned Cole Sherman an impressive professional reputation. That reputation has grown over the years, beyond the borders of Toronto, to private and public sector clients in every field.

A GOOD BALANCE

Unlike many firms in the industry today, URS Cole Sherman has managed to create a balance between private and public sector clients by offering an unprecedented level of service. "A cornerstone of our management philosophy is to ensure we understand our clients' and their stakeholders' needs and constraints," says Murray Thompson, Executive Vice-President and Director of Operations.

The company's responsiveness to stakeholders' needs derives, in part, from its extensive experience with the public sector, where public needs and accountability are the

Cole, Sherman & Associates Limited led a multidisciplinary team for a unique project to dismantle the East end of the elevated Gardiner Expressway in downtown Toronto.

Cole Sherman has provided urban development consulting services for more than 5,000 acres throughout the Greater Toronto Area.

Cole Sherman designed and managed the construction of its main office in Thornhill, Ontario.

priorities. URS Cole Sherman has a solid reputation for technical excellence and integrity in both the public and the private sector. Multitalented and flexible staff provide a full range of engineering and architectural services.

The Thornhill office has an energetic atmosphere that comes from the company's ambitious and skilled young engineers and architects who can see the opportunities the firm has to offer, balanced by the technical soundness and experience of the senior staff. Long before dot-coms were credited with inventing a less formal approach to business organization, URS Cole Sherman had already fostered a system of flat organization—a close family culture where every member is valued. Ideas are considered no matter who suggests them or how long that individual has been with the company. As far as Cole is concerned, it is this atmosphere that has kept staff loyal and the business exciting, innovative, and fresh.

The fact that the business is growing serves as a testament to the company's record of success. Many major cities, including Toronto, were conceived before the beginning of the last century and are having to redesign their traffic systems, rethink their transportation networks, overhaul their water and sewage treatment plants, and rewire their buildings. The energetic and dynamic staff at Cole, Sherman & Associates Limited is enjoying this new expansion era in infrastructure. The Cole Sherman team addresses issues head-on and looks forward to exciting new challenges. ◆

Design of the reconfiguration of Queen Elizabeth Way and Erin Mills Parkway to handle increased traffic volumes involved complex staging to maintain traffic flow throughout the two-year construction period.

Cole Sherman won an Award of Merit from the Toronto Historical Board for "retention and restoration design" of Metropolitan Gray Coach Bus Terminal on Bay Street.

EIDLER GRINNELL PARTNERSHIP/ARCHITECTS (FORMERLY ZEIDLER Roberts Partnership/Architects) developed from a small Ontario architectural practice that had its beginnings in 1880 in Peterborough, Ontario, and moved to Toronto in 1954. Now a globally recognized practice, the firm has a staff of 140 in its

Toronto headquarters and offices in London, Berlin, and West Palm Beach. The Partnership's expertise covers virtually the full range of architectural, urban, and interior design services.

The firm is recognized in Toronto for its acclaimed designs of Ontario Place and the Toronto Eaton Centre, which rank with Niagara Falls as Ontario's top tourist destinations. Many people from Ontario and across Canada have experienced a visit to the Partnership's Hospital for Sick Children's Atrium, the Canadian Cancer Institute/Princess Margaret Hospital, the Sunnybrook Health Science Centre Clinical Services Wing, the Toronto Centre for the Arts, or the Mississauga Living Arts Centre.

The Partnership's renovation of the historic Queen's Quay Terminal into a delightful mix of shopping, theatre, office, and condominium uses was a signal that Toronto's waterfront could be charming, and compelling. The firm's National Trade Centre revitalized the entrance to the Canadian National

Exhibition grounds, redefining its main processional route through the Princes' Gates, while restoring the venerable coliseum.

On top of Zeidler Grinnell's strong portfolio in health care, performing arts, exhibition facilities, and retail complexes, the firm has constructed an example of almost every building type.

INTERNATIONAL REPUTATION

The firm's international reputation for excellence blossomed with the opening of the Hamilton, Ontario, McMaster University Health Sciences Centre. Called "obsolescence-proof" by architectural critics, the hospital's design allowed for unpredictable future changes to medical facility requirements. Accessible interstitial floors were created to carry the building's mechanical systems, allowing for conversion and expansion at any time without interrupting hospital operations.

In Canada, the Zeidler Grinnell Partnership has completed more than 150 projects; many have become community landmarks, such as: British Columbia's Canada Place in Vancouver; Alberta's Walter C. Mackenzie Health Sciences Centre in Edmonton; Ontario's Canadian Red Cross Society National Office in Ottawa; Quebec's Place Montréal Trust in Montreal; and New Brunswick's Saint John Regional Hospital.

Over the past several decades, Zeidler Grinnell has been making

its mark abroad with a number of high-profile projects, which have often been won through international competitions. Cinedom in MediaPark, Cologne, has proved since it opened to be Germany's most financially successful cinema; as well, it has been crowned by its patrons as the world's most comfortable theatre.

Much of the Partnership's design prowess can be seen in the soon-to-be-completed Torre Mayor office tower in Mexico City. The country's tallest structure will rise 55 storeys over the capital. The peaking glass-and-stone façade, as well as the dramatic cutback through the lower floors, creates a dazzling entrance from the street-level plaza.

The Raymond F. Kravis Center for the Performing Arts in West Palm Beach has become a stunning landmark in the state of Florida. Its grand staircase behind a glass wall makes the life of the theatre visible to all, and becomes especially glamorous at night.

Other noteworthy American projects include Baltimore's Columbus Center of Marine Biotechnology, The Gallery at Harborplace and University of Maryland's Homer Gudelsky Building, Philadelphia's Liberty Place and Ritz-Carlton Hotel, and the Detroit Receiving Hospital.

Major Pacific Rim projects include BNI City in Jakarta, The Mall in Kuala Lumpur, and the Furama Hotel in Hong Kong.

The firm has grown over the year

In Canada alone, Zeidler Grinnell Partnership/Architects has completed more than 150 projects; many have become community landmarks, such as British Columbia's Canada Place in Vancouver.

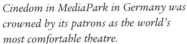

Cinedom in MediaPark in Germany was crowned by its patrons as the world's most comfortable theatre.

GEORG MÜLLER

LENSCAPE INC.

with the addition of partners, associate partners, and associates. Eberhard Zeidler was joined as a Senior Partner by Ian Grinnell in 1987. Alan Munn became a Senior Partner in early 2001, when the firm name was updated to the Zeidler Grinnell Partnership.

Many of the partners and senior staff have also been with the firm for decades. Each has helped to expand the firm's portfolio into its present diverse range of project types. As well, with a veteran partner heading each project, clients benefit from his or her personal touch.

Today, Zeidler Grinnell remains expert in reacting to the changing global marketplace, having assembled a staff whose breadth of cultural backgrounds flourishes in the global design market.

The firm's culture of innovation and excellence in design has resulted in a formidable portfolio of built work. The principles of synthesizing emotional and functional needs into a seamless whole result in buildings that are places where people want to be—buildings owners are proud to call their own.

The firm has been recognized with more than 100 national and international awards, including five prestigious Governor General's Medals for Architecture, four Massey Medals for Outstanding Canadian Architecture, eight Awards of Excellence from *Canadian Architect*, and three Ontario Association of Architect (OAA) Awards, including the 1999 OAA 25-Year Award for Ontario Place.

Senior Partner Eberhard Zeidler has been recognized for his contribution to Canadian architecture with many honours, including the prestigious Royal Architectural Institute of Canada's Gold Medal, the Order of Canada, and the Order of Ontario.

General Partners with the firm include Don Vetere, Gerald Stein, Francis Kwok, Jurgen Henze, and Tarek El-Khatib. Senior Associate Partners are Dalibor Vokac and Rob Eley. Associate Partners are Andrea Richardson, Stuart Mussells, Ron Nemeth, Barbara Hopewell, George Friedman, Lyndon Devaney, and Vaidila Banelis. Director of the Berlin office is Thomas Hübener and Director of the Florida office is Mike Nelson.

Zeidler Grinnell's complete portfolio can be viewed on-line at www.zgpa.com. To really get a feel for the work of the Partnership however, one must surely visit and experience one of Zeidler Grinnell Partnership/Architects' buildings. 🍁

Clockwise from top left:
The Columbus Center of Marine Biotechnology in Baltimore was a winner of a 1997 Canadian Governor General's Medal for Architecture.

Many people from Ontario and across Canada have experienced a visit to the Partnership's Hospital for Sick Children's Atrium.

Torre Mayor in Mexico City, the country's tallest structure, will rise 55 storeys over the capital city.

CARLOS DINIZ

AGF MANAGEMENT LIMITED PROVES A FUND COMPANY CAN BE INNOvative, creative, and successful. AGF is one of Canada's largest and best-known mutual fund and investment companies, helping Canadians realize their financial dreams. With more than $34 billion in managed assets, AGF serves investors

through a broad range of award-winning funds and retirement solutions.

Back in 1957, company cofounders Allan Manford and C. Warren Goldring had a unique and revolutionary vision to pool the funds of Canadian investors to allow them greater access to the U.S. market through the New York Stock Exchange. The fund became known as the American Growth Fund, the first fund of U.S. equities available to Canadian investors.

And AGF was born. Using the initials from the name of the first fund, the company grew quickly and became known for breakthrough funds and top-notch investment performance. In 1970, AGF became the first Canadian fund company to offer a mutual fund of Japanese equities and, in 1996, became the first Canadian company to establish a fund that specializes in investment in China.

AGF is a global company with a Canadian home. In Canada, AGF has offices in Halifax, Montreal, Toronto, Calgary, and Vancouver. To ensure a global focus, the company maintains a team of advisers and portfolio management teams headquartered in the key foreign markets of London, Dublin, and Singapore. AGF also maintains offices in Tokyo and Beijing.

Blake Goldring serves as President and Chief Executive Officer of AGF Management Limited.

HELPING INVESTORS REACH THEIR DREAMS

AGF poses the question "What are you doing after work?" to highlight the company's dedication to helping Canadians reach any destination or goal throughout their lives. The company is the choice of more than 1 million Canadians who invest in AGF's well-diversified family of mutual funds, the Harmony wrap program, and AGF Magna Vista Private Investment Management.

With more than 70 mutual funds, AGF investors can choose from a wide range of domestic, international, and specialty mutual funds that use a variety of investment objectives

and management styles in a broad spectrum of markets.

AN ORIGINAL VISION: A DISTINCTIVE BRAND

AGF is distinctive as one of the only mutual fund companies in Canada that has built a unique brand. Not only is the AGF tiger one of the most recognized corporate symbols in Canada, but the company has also created one of the most popular advertising campaigns in the investment industry. AGF's advertising features celebrated pop cultural icons such as Spiderman, Santa Claus, and Gumby and Pokey planning their retirement dreams.

In 2000, AGF took a major stake in a new television series, *Moneyworld*, and a companion Web site as an innovative, new way to harness the best in financial information. *Moneyworld* combines finance with media in a unique program offering insights on trends

and patterns, as well as news developments. The Internet site offers streaming video updates from the floor of major stock exchanges and from Reuters' bureaus around the globe.

AGF's original vision also shines through in its corporate giving. The company is well-known for its symbol of a Sumatran tiger, a species now endangered in the wild. AGF invests in the work of the World Wildlife Fund (WWF) and supports a number of initiatives to protect the Sumatran tiger. The company supports the Toronto Zoo as well, helping to fund habitat improvement and tiger research. In addition, AGF is a sponsor of the major Canadian film festivals in Montreal, Toronto, Calgary, and Vancouver.

Since 1957, AGF Management Limited has helped Canadians realize their dreams, and the company fully intends to pursue this vision well into the future. ♦

▲ © JUDY NISENHOLT

1960
1974

1962   Toronto French School

1965   Goodman and Carr LLP

1966   Seneca College of Applied Arts and
Technology

1967   Humber College

1968   Anixter Canada Inc.

1968   Courtesy Chev Olds Ltd.

1971   Deep Foundations Contractors Inc.

1972   Metrus Properties Limited

1974   CanWest Global Communications Corp.

1974   Rex Pak Limited

1974   Tim Hortons

ONNAISSANCE EST FORCE [KNOWLEDGE IS STRENGTH] IS THE MOTTO of the highly respected Toronto French School (TFS), one of the largest independent schools in Canada. TFS offers bilingual, co-educational learning for students from prekindergarten through university entrance. ❧ Since its inception in 1962,

TFS has evolved from premises located in a small house to a school that welcomes more than 1,200 students on two campuses, one in Mississauga and the other in Toronto. The main campus is located on 28 wooded acres in central Toronto. This beautiful ravine setting is home to students from prekindergarten (age three) to high school. The school's newly renovated Mississauga campus welcomes students from prekindergarten to high school entrance, and is ideally located for easy commuting access.

In its relatively short history, TFS has acquired a reputation as a leader and innovator in education. With bilingualism, an international perspective, and a very enriched curriculum, TFS is unique in its offerings.

While some 90 percent of students join TFS with little or no background in French, the school's graduates are fully bilingual. Students may also learn German or Latin as early as grade six, and start Spanish and classical Greek in high school.

Toronto French School offers bilingual, co-educational learning for students from prekindergarten through university entrance.

INTERNATIONAL PERSPECTIVE

Undertaken in the last two years of high school, the International Baccalaureate (IB) Diploma provides TFS students with excellent academic skills and a valuable credential for entry into major universities around the world. TFS prepares this prestigious

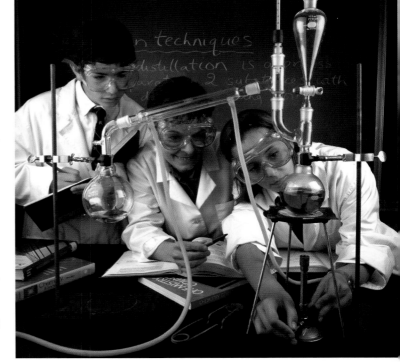

academic program bilingually, in both English and French. The IB Diploma success rate of TFS students consistently exceeds the international average, and students who achieve strong marks in IB higher level courses are regularly offered advanced placement or transfer credits by universities.

The high standards of the French program are recognized by the French Ministry of Education up to Grade 10. Students have the option of writing a French national exam, the Diplôme

National du Brevet des Collèges. The program is an effective means of evaluating TFS candidates within a network of accredited French schools throughout the world. The exam results of TFS students confirm their high level of fluency.

School faculty hail from more than 20 nations, and TFS students themselves represent more than 40 nationalities. An international background gives students a competitive edge in Canadian national competitions, as well as in international competitions like the Royal Commonwealth Essay Competition and the Model United Nations.

ENRICHED CURRICULUM

Toronto French School's distinctive feature is its enriched curriculum. The school embraces an interdisciplinary approach that extends beyond traditional academic parameters and aims to address the needs of the whole child.

The Toronto French School prepares its students to pursue post-secondary studies at the university of their choice, preparing them for the future. ❧

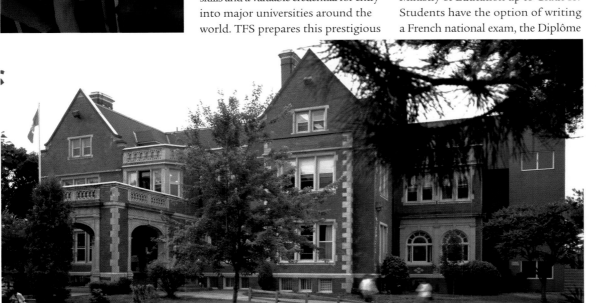

ETRUS PROPERTIES LIMITED IS ONE OF THE BEST-KNOWN NAMES in the development business of the Greater Toronto Area. Serving clients of all sizes is the company's specialty—from microbusinesses to Fortune 500 companies, Metrus understands bricks and mortar. Metrus Properties' home base is in

the Vaughn area, nestled among its own tenants, but the company works on major projects across Canada and the United States. Metrus owns and manages more than 10 million square feet of property in three principal areas: industrial, office, and retail.

Metrus Properties is a proud member of the Con-Drain team, a unique group of nine specialized companies. The companies include sewer and water main construction, road building, underground utility installation, residential home building, and land development.

Founded in 1972 by the DeGasperis brothers, the Con-Drain team has played a crucial role in the modern development of southern Ontario. Metrus is run by Robert DeGasperis, representing the company's second generation of DeGasperis development and construction professionals.

ONE-STOP SERVICE

What makes Metrus unique in a very competitive market is its relationship with Con-Drain. As part of a comprehensive team, Metrus can offer its clients one-stop-shopping service—a very unique capability in Canada. In concert with the Con-Drain team, Metrus can take a client through every aspect of land development, which includes everything from planning and construction to leasing and management. Metrus can bring clients a truly turnkey solution to the most complex of building needs.

Metrus also offers the advantage of owning a huge range of properties, from very small to very large—a broad existing portfolio that gives customers immediate location availability. Metrus' land banks are ready to go, and the skills to service land are available with just a quick call to the Con-Drain Group.

Over the years, Metrus has developed a reputation for being able to get things done quickly. The company's connection to a network means that many services can be done in-house, which provides considerable efficiency and cost savings

to clients. As a result, Metrus has built a significant business with clients among Canada's leading companies, including the country's big-six banks, Magna, Lego, Wal-Mart, Citibank, Quebecor, and Sherwin Williams.

HIGHEST QUALITY

In addition to the capability of one-stop shopping, clients are drawn to Metrus because of its unwavering commitment to quality. Quality has always been a family philosophy in this privately held firm, resulting in long-term relationships with clients. Because of the family orientation of the company, clients deal—and work—directly with the leaders of the firm.

The company considers itself a very hands-on developer, able and

interested in being there at every step of the building process. Metrus' strong relationships extend well beyond the firm's direct clients. In the development industry, good relationships with all levels of government are critical to success. A dedication to quality and a passion for going beyond mandated standards have helped to strengthen that key relationship for Metrus.

Business has been growing steadily every year since Metrus Properties Limited's inception. The company has found the recipe for leadership in development: commitment to quality, turnkey solutions, and good working relationships. This foundation will ensure that Metrus will have as bright a future as its clients. ◆

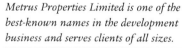

Metrus Properties Limited is one of the best-known names in the development business and serves clients of all sizes.

GOODMAN AND CARR LLP IS NOT A TRADITIONAL LAW FIRM. GO DIFFERENT is Goodman and Carr LLP's recruiting slogan. A firm that has the ability to think outside the box, Goodman and Carr LLP recognizes where its strengths lie and excels in those areas, believing it is the firm for the entrepreneur.

Clearly, Goodman and Carr LLP has pulled away from the pack of downtown Toronto Bay Street law firms. Established in 1965, the full-service firm has undergone unprecedented change and growth in recent years, while maintaining its core strengths. One of Canada's leading law firms, Goodman and Carr LLP has more than 30 practice groups, and focusses its talents through its four main practice areas: business, litigation, real estate, and tax. The firm has one of the most entrepreneurial and sophisticated corporate finance practices in the country.

The firm's business law practice area focusses on a wide range of transactions, from mergers and acquisitions to complex financings. Litigation has an emphasis on commercial litigation, but includes more esoteric areas of expertise, such as class action litigation and assisting victims of sexual assault. The real estate group handles all aspects of purchasing, selling, and financing real property. The firm's large commercial leasing practice is one of the foremost in Canada. The widely respected tax section provides everything from corporate and personal planning to tax litigation.

In the past decade, Goodman and Carr LLP has honed its expertise in venture capital, information technology, health care, and financial

Established in 1965, the full-service law firm of Goodman and Carr LLP has undergone unprecedented change and growth while maintaining its core strengths.

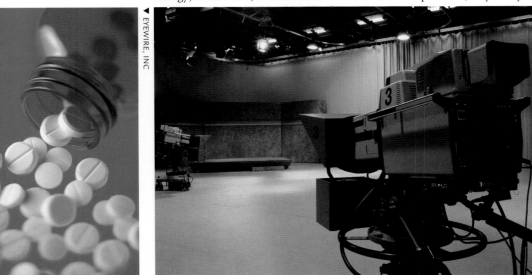

services. The firm has also created new and growing practice areas.

CREATIVE THINKING

The *Financial Post* has referred to Goodman and Carr LLP as being "frequently creative," and the firm itself virtually vibrates with creative energy. "We define ourselves not by our pedigree, but by our new ideas, our new best practices," says Gary

Luftspring, Managing Partner.

The Goodman and Carr LLP culture is strongly entrepreneurial. One strategy for the future that provides evidence of the GO DIFFERENT slogan includes partnering with others like Bryker Technology Partners, a joint venture capital fund with a mandate to finance start-up entrepreneurial businesses. Bryker finances early-stage Internet companies in e-commerce software development, or offers services in the business-to-business, business-to-consumer, and consumer-to-consumer marketplace. Luftspring recognized that the niche market in the small to mid-sized e-commerce start-up areas, which is Bryker's specialty, would synergize perfectly with Goodman and Carr LLP's venture capital start-up expertise.

ENTREPRENEURIAL SPIRIT

Partnerships led by outside experts, like Bryker Technology Partners, allow the partners at Goodman and Carr LLP to reap the benefit of synergistic business enterprises without having to leave their active legal

EYEWIRE, INC

EYEWIRE, INC

In the past decade, Goodman and Carr LLP has honed its expertise in venture capital, information technology, health care, financial services, and sports, entertainment & media practices.

practices—a unique opportunity in the legal industry. Within the firm and its partnering affiliation, the entrepreneurial spirit reigns supreme.

"We are seriously committed to demonstrating our entrepreneurial energies," explains Luftspring. "We are continually looking for opportunities. We are eager to compete in other industries, and we understand that looking at legal services too narrowly will be the industry's downfall." Goodman and Carr LLP is intent on discovering new and innovative ways to add value to the services the firm provides to clients. Human resources services and wealth management services, for example, have been creatively and successfully expanded since 1998.

Goodman and Carr LLP has worked particularly hard to anticipate and meet new clients' needs, as well as identifying dynamic business opportunities in various markets. While identifying new markets is im-

portant to the firm, it should also be noted that Goodman and Carr LLP has a strong commitment to maintaining and strengthening ongoing and long-time client relationships. The firm places a high value on working to strengthen existing relationships with clients, while continuing to work toward finding new ways to best assist these clients.

Some of the best-known lawyers in the legal industry have been lured to Goodman and Carr LLP because of its growing reputation for entrepreneurial business and the creative spirit of the firm. One member best sums it up as "one of the best places to work in Toronto."

GLOBAL FLEXIBILITY

Located in downtown Toronto, Goodman and Carr LLP is proud of its rapidly growing global client base. The firm's size and single location offer key competitive advantages—the most important of

which is its flexibility.

Goodman and Carr LLP's creativity and entrepreneurial expertise give the firm a leading edge, which is placing the firm at the forefront of its field. Goodman and Carr LLP is prepared to meet new demands with speed and agility, and the firm's business sense is firmly entrenched in its culture, while its partners and members are continually being inspired by meeting these many new challenges.

"We are ready and willing to try new things," says Luftspring. "We have to be exceptionally flexible for our clients and, furthermore, we really enjoy doing things that other firms aren't doing. Goodman and Carr is a firm focussed on coming up with new ideas and following them through." And that, in essence, is what Goodman and Carr LLP believes sets it apart from the competition, and what ultimately will ensure continued success and growth in the future. 🍁

▶ EYEWIRE, INC.

One of Canada's leading law firms, Goodman and Carr LLP has more than 30 practice groups, and focusses its talents through its four main practice areas: business, litigation, real estate, and tax.

ITH AN EYE ON THE EMERGING OPPORTUNITIES OF TODAY'S economy, Seneca College of Applied Arts and Technology provides students with the tools they need for success now and well into the 21st century. The largest college in Canada, with eight campuses conveniently located throughout the

Greater Toronto area, Seneca offers a tremendous variety of class sizes and methods of teaching—from in-class lectures and on-line learning to co-op and field placements.

Seneca's size and diversity allow for dynamic partnerships with industry leaders, the latest in hands-on computer technology, extensive student services, academic advisement and career counseling, and exceptional financial support through awards, scholarships, bursaries, and loans.

Seneca's campus of advanced technology, Seneca@York, opened its doors in September 1999.

CAREERS FOR THE REAL WORLD

Seneca offers students challenging, innovative programs geared to careers in the global workplace. Every program is backed by high academic standards and excellent professional faculty, and many have opportunities for students to gain valuable work experience through co-op and work-placement programs. Students can choose from more than 260 career options in fields such as applied arts, business, health sciences, and technology.

Leading areas of study at Seneca include biotechnology and pharmaceutical studies, business, computer

sciences, and health sciences. Programs that are recognized both nationally and internationally include accounting and finance, aviation flight technology, electronic engineering, fire protection, international business and marketing, and three-D digital animation.

Since 1967, Seneca College has provided a foundation of success for such notable alumni as Canadian Senator Vivienne Poy, Magna International Vice President of Human Resources Marc Neeb, Air Canada pilot Daniel Fuchs, and Global Television news anchor Beverly Thomson.

"When I went to Seneca, there was a real sense of experimentation, newness, and a great community spirit," says Seneca business administration alumnus Val Azzoli, cochairman/co-CEO of Atlantic Records in New York. "The business principles I learned then are the same ones I use today."

MEETING THE NEEDS OF THE GLOBAL MARKETPLACE

With the largest enrollment of international students attending college in Canada, and more than 75 countries represented in Seneca's student population, the college embodies the cultural mosaic that makes up the rich diversity of Toronto.

Seneca's strong international reputation has attracted the attention

of educational institutions worldwide, resulting in agreements to utilize Seneca curricula in classrooms throughout Europe, Pacific Asia, and Latin America. Joint programs and transfer agreements with universities and other colleges in Canada and around the world provide the opportunity for students to earn both a diploma and a degree. This gives students a flexible and affordable option to combine the strengths of applied education and theoretical learning. Seneca has agreements with such institutions as University of Guelph, York University, Embry-Riddle Aeronautical University in Florida, D'Youville College in New York, and the University of Western Sydney in Australia.

STRATEGIC ALLIANCES WITH INDUSTRY LEADERS

Corporate partnerships give Seneca access to emerging trends and changing technology. This allows Seneca the opportunity to create and adapt programs in anticipation of workplace needs of the future. Students benefit from having training in the latest trends and key business solutions before they graduate.

In partnership with Orad Hi-Tec Systems and Silicon Graphics, Seneca is the first educational institution in North America to offer virtual set technology training in a television broadcasting program. Another partner,

Students in Seneca's School of Communication Arts work with the latest in broadcast technology, receiving hands-on training in leading industry equipment and techniques.

Aglient Technologies Canada Inc., has supplied Seneca with training labs that feature the leading-edge pharmaceutical laboratory equipment used in the industry. Seneca's other corporate partners include IBM Canada Ltd., Oracle Corporation Canada Inc., mBanx, Cisco Systems, Xerox, Lucent Technologies, CIBC, and Netscape Canada.

Seneca College is committed to the ongoing development of academic programs and industry partnerships that give students an education focussed on the global opportunities of the future. To ensure that this commitment is met, every Seneca program is designed and continually developed with the guidance of academic advisory councils comprised of professionals with relevant industry experience.

CAMPUSES FOR A UNIQUE CITY

Seneca's campuses offer a variety of learning environments and educational opportunities by which to experience Toronto. The Newnham Campus houses programs in applied arts and business—in fact, Seneca has the largest business faculty in Canada. The English Language Institute provides English language instruction to international students, and has a global reputation for innovation and success in its

approach to teaching. The campus also offers a 1,107-bed residence and conference centre.

Seneca's King Campus offers a beautiful country setting for programs in applied health sciences, recreation, and law enforcement. Located on 282 hectares of woods, lake, and fields, students can enjoy a unique learning environment that also features a 233-bed residence and the Eaton Hall Inn and Conference Centre.

Students at the open-access Yorkgate Campus can select self-paced learning with customized programs in academic upgrading and office systems. New students can register on any Monday.

Don Mills Campus is the fully wired, high-tech home for Seneca's computer networking and computer systems programs. Students have access to some of the latest computer equipment in Canada.

Seneca's campus of advanced technology, Seneca@York, provides the educational resources and leading-edge technology to address the need for knowledge-based workers in the global economy of the 21st century. The campus is home to Seneca's Schools of Computer Studies, Communication Arts, and Biological Science and Applied Chemistry, as well as the Centre for Professional Communications.

With a commitment to creating a dynamic learning and working environment, offering excellence in education, and building strong relationships with the college's students, partners, and community, Seneca College is preparing today's students for tomorrow's careers. ❦

Seneca College of Applied Arts and Technology's Learning Commons is a learning space outside the classroom that brings the traditional library into the 21st century with key resources, equipment, and personnel.

I N SURVEY AFTER SURVEY, STUDENTS AND EMPLOYERS RANK HUMBER College of Applied Arts and Technology as the best community college in Toronto. Located in the lush Humber Valley of Toronto since 1967, Humber has the highest application rate in Ontario, enrolling some 12,000 full-time and more than 60,000 part-time students every year.

Year after year, Canadian and international students choose Humber for its dedication to exceptional education.

At Humber, students choose from more than 135 full-time programs at the post-secondary and postgraduate diploma level, and more than 1,000 continuing education programs. By concentrating on being the best college it can be, Humber has also become one of Canada's biggest.

DYNAMIC INNOVATION

Humber's popularity comes as no surprise, as the college has proactively created one of the most dynamic program rosters in the country. Humber is the only Canadian institution to be invited to join the League for Innovation in the Community College, a U.S.-based consortium of international colleges organized to stimulate experimentation and innovation in all areas of college development.

As well, the college has been selected as a Vanguard Learning College. An international evaluation committee recently named Humber College as the only Canadian institute to become a member of the select group of 12—recognizing Humber's outstanding record of achievement in learning-centred education. As a Vanguard Learning College, Humber College will act as an incubator and catalyst for the growth of educational models and practices.

As a member of these two prestigious groups, Humber remains focussed on moving beyond the traditional role of the community college to become a college where dynamic thought, non-linear thinking, and innovative solutions drive education in new directions.

"Humber College's programs are renowned for their innovative and unique approach," says Dr. Robert Gordon, President of Humber College. "At the same time, we are committed to respecting our roots and our values that have been effective for more than 30 years."

Clockwise from top:
Located in the lush Humber Valley of Toronto, Humber College of Applied Arts and Technology has the highest application rate in Ontario.

Humber graduates study programs and courses designed to be market responsive.

Year after year, Canadian and international students choose Humber for its dedication to exceptional education.

One can easily begin to understand how this blend of dynamism and innovation, combined with a respect for the college's past, creates a very successful place of learning.

RESPONSIVE EDUCATION

For decades now, Humber has worked in concert with faculty and employers to design programs and courses that are market responsive. Key relationships are developed and maintained, strategically placing college leaders in a position to respond to industry needs. The Digital Image Training Centre at Humber's North Campus, for instance, is an award-winning facility that teaches the latest applications in digital photography, three-D modelling, Internet design, and audiovisual production. The Digital Imaging Training Centre

meets the needs of Toronto's learners seeking digital knowledge.

The Canadian Plastics Training Centre (CPTC) has also worked in concert with industry, labour, and government to create the primary resource for timely, practical solutions. Since 1993, CPTC has certified hundreds of operators and technicians, working both at the campus and in-plant with industry giants such as Magna, Husky, and Toyota.

Humber's commitment to education keeps on growing. In the near future, Humber is planning to introduce integrated programs that will enable students to earn both a college diploma and a university degree in just four years. The groundbreaking project will see the forces of Humber join with the University of Guelph, one of the province's

leading universities. The Humber-Guelph Centre for Advanced Education and Training will seamlessly integrate the degree and diploma experience with significantly lower economic and time investments. Faculty will be drawn from both educational pools of talent.

Students accepted into the brand new College of e will also experience the best Humber has to offer. A Microsoft Certified Centre for Excellence in e-commerce, the College of e will fall under the umbrella of advanced information technology, focussing on business-to-business and business-to-consumer markets. Humber joins Microsoft and the Microsoft Solution Providers, such as SAP, Dell, and Macromedia, to provide the educational tools necessary to fuel the programs. It is only through this type of responsive education that industry will be able to fill the demand for trained people.

FUTURE PATHWAYS

As society continues to change, so do the educational needs of Torontonians and the world. For almost four decades, Humber has engaged industry professionals in advisory roles. Nurturing these relationships has helped Humber establish a path from its past to its future.

One example of moving forward along the educational pathway is the relationship that Humber has formed with DaimlerChrysler. A few years ago, DaimlerChrysler approached Humber to meet its corporate training goals by creating a unique degree-granting program for the company's employees.

The college jumped at the chance to partner with this automotive industry leader, creating a program specific to DaimlerChrysler. Taking into account prior learning, DaimlerChrysler's employees were recognized for past experiences and training, an important factor in lifelong learning models. Further, employees could realistically participate if the schedule was flexible and worked around their 24-hour rotational shift work, which meant creating learning centres at the plant. The result? To the joy of everyone involved, enrolment numbers exceeded expectations. Soon Humber will be congratulating the first set of graduates—who, through traditional

models, may not have been able to further their education. It is this commitment to lifelong learning that is so important to Toronto and the world.

Walking through the halls of Humber, one cannot help but notice the mosaic of people. Those fresh out of high school and university mix with those returning to update skills, as well as with international students looking for an exceptional educational experience. As student and industry needs evolve, so too will Humber evolve and innovate, and because of this, it will remain Toronto's preeminent centre for education and training. 🍁

Clockwise from top:
Humber's Lakeshore Campus is an educational jewel nestled in the heart of Toronto, Canada's largest business and entertainment centre.

Humber students can choose from more than 135 full-time programs at the post-secondary and postgraduate diploma level, and more than 1,000 continuing education programs.

Humber's popularity with students increases as the college proactively creates one of the most dynamic program rosters in the country.

A Microsoft Certified Centre for Excellence in e-commerce, the brand new College of e will fall under the umbrella of advanced information technology, focussing on business-to-business and business-to-consumer markets.

ANIXTER CANADA INC.

ANIXTER CANADA INC.'S CABLING THREADS THROUGH ALMOST EVERY major business in Toronto, as well as many of the minor ones. One of the world's largest suppliers of data, communications, and electrical cabling, Anixter has more than 170 sales and service locations in some 40 countries and more than 5,000 employees worldwide. Anixter stocks more than 70,000 miles of cable in North America alone, which is enough cable to circle the equator twice, go through the centre of the earth three times, and tie a large knot with the remaining 80 miles.

In Toronto, Anixter is a major player with a significant national hub in Mississauga. Established in Canada in 1968, Anixter is now in every major city across the nation with hubs in Edmonton, Toronto, and Montreal. The company's national warehousing capabilities are extraordinary—Anixter has more than 700,000 square feet of warehouse space, and capacity is constantly growing.

In Canada, Anixter operates in three key markets: wire and cable (electrical), communications from copper to fiber cabling, and public networks. Distribution reaches virtually all industries across the country, including both large and small businesses.

"SERVICE IS OUR TECHNOLOGY"

Since its inception, Anixter has excelled at distribution, logistics, and inventory management. The combination of a state-of-the-art inventory management system, global distribution network, vast inventory, and willingness to customize logistics programs has allowed Anixter to cultivate long-term partnerships with customers and suppliers.

Anixter calls its management process Anixter Integrated Supply; in fact, the process constitutes an entire division of the company. Essentially, Anixter Integrated Supply takes the traditional buy-sell relationship to the next level. Anixter looks at the business and logistics processes through which products flow by analyzing procurement, inventory management, and product development to create the most efficient, cost-effective system for each individual customer.

Using this integrated supply approach has several key advantages for customers: the process reduces cost, improves customer service, allows companies to focus on their core competencies, increases flexibility, improves scalability, and optimizes personnel and capital expenditures. The advantages to using Anixter itself include the firm's worldwide distribution and logistics capabilities, local Canadian resources, single computer network, and extensive product knowledge. Anixter is a company wholly structured to its commitment to help customers through the entire supply chain process.

A crucial part of good service is a good product. For example, there was no method of distinguishing the quality of data cable until 1989, when Anixter devised its levels rating system that became the model for industry standards. Anixter requires that all cable taken into levels inventory exceed all international cable standards.

Anixter Canada Inc. is a leading Canadian company with exceptional products, service, and performance.

GROWTH IN CANADA

In the late 1960s, the Anixter team recognized the need and potential in the Canadian market. The market was growing and evolving in step with the United States, and the need for communications systems was growing apace. Canadian companies needed communications systems that would not fail, and that could handle change and growth. Businesses were looking for a company that could provide consistency and confidence; Anixter delivered, and soon there were local operations in every major Canadian city.

While parts of the global company have grown through acquisition, Anixter's Canadian growth and expansion have been created by sales, which speaks to the continually expanding need for the company's quality and service. From 1998 to 2001, due to rising demand, Anixter increased its Canadian warehouse space by 1,000 square feet a month.

One of Anixter's recent expansions was the creation of the Anixter hub in the central Mississauga area. The clean lines of Anixter's warehouse reflect the simplicity of the supply chains the company creates for its customers. Inside the vast warehouse, with shelves going back great distances, friendly Anixter staff members take orders as small as 10 phone jacks and as large as the cabling for an entire subdivision.

A CARING COMPANY

Toronto-area Anixter employees have an exceptional amount of enthusiasm for charitable causes. The last Friday of every month is a dedicated charitable dress-down day. Employees have worn red for the Heart and Stroke Foundation, denim for breast cancer research, and daffodils for cancer. Employees have a role in choosing each month's charitable cause, and their choices are heartily supported by management, which results in a very high level of participation.

Anixter's most significant charitable efforts have gone toward raising funds for Toronto's Hospital for Sick Children. The company's annual golf tournament, Play for the Kids, raises thousands of dollars every year. Anixter's employees, executives, customers, and suppliers all participate in the daylong event.

Anixter Canada Inc.'s friendly enthusiasm in its charitable work is a reflection of the energy and commitment the firm brings to serving its customers' needs. As a leading Canadian company with exceptional products, service, and performance, Anixter is part of what has kept the Canadian market a great success. 🍁

In Toronto, Anixter is a major player with a significant national hub in Mississauga and national warehousing capabilities with more than 700,000 square feet of space.

COURTESY CHEV OLDS LTD.

COURTESY CHEV OLDS LTD.

A LOCAL LANDMARK SINCE 1968, COURTESY CHEV OLDS LTD. DOES not look at all like a typical car dealership. With its vaulted roofs, cobblestoned patio, tiered displays, and immaculate lawns and flowers, Courtesy could be taken for a beautiful civic centre were it not for all the new cars parked

neatly around the perimeter. Inside, natural woods and deep colors add warmth to the main showroom, while a bright secondary showroom—located a floor below—holds 40 vehicles for display and delivery. Not surprisingly, this unique facility won an architectural award for its unusual profile and design.

Like the company, its president, Don Polyschuk, is also one of a kind. A consummate car man, he began in an entry-level position right out of high school some 35 years ago and has not looked back since. A student of the business who loves his product, Polyschuk consumes car magazines and trade publications, and travels regularly to auto shows and design centers across the United States. He prides himself on knowing everything about each new model, and is usually first out of the office to see them when the transport truck arrives.

Polyschuk has customized cars, modified trucks, entered convertibles in parades, and held sales in tents, warehouses, and shopping malls. He has sponsored countless local sports teams, given a car to a needy family, and even taught college marketing classes—all to keep fun in the business, give back to the

With its vaulted roofs, cobblestoned patio, tiered displays, and immaculate lawns and flowers, Courtesy Chev Olds Ltd. could be taken for a beautiful civic centre.

community, and ensure Courtesy's name is out there.

Most of all, this dealer has always wanted to be first; not just in sales, but first to try something new— ideas that will change the game and produce a better experience for his customers. Recently honoured by General Motors for celebrating 25 years as a GM dealer, Polyschuk is still as enthusiastic about the business and determined to break new ground as he ever was. "I'm tenacious, hardworking, and I love what I do," he says, explaining his success and longevity in a highly competitive business.

HOME OF THE "ONLY PRICE"

Hassle-free, one-price selling made headlines in 1993 when Polyschuk took a bold step to eliminate negotiating from the car buying process at Courtesy. "Customers were asking us to please just tell them the price, right up front," he says of the decision. "And as soon as we posted our best price–our 'Only Price'–on every windshield, our relationship with our customers and our whole company's culture changed. And it's been an overwhelming success ever since."

By GM's numbers, Courtesy ranks among the highest in the country for customer satisfaction. Ask anyone why, and employees invariably talk about the Only Price philosophy. "We've taken the emphasis off making deals and focussed on making sure our customers get the best value for their money," says one veteran salesperson. "We aren't pushy—we respect them, listen, and help them make their decision." Courtesy's long-standing 48-hour money-back guarantee allows customers to change their minds and further relieves the pressure around making a purchase.

ON THE QUEENSWAY

If Courtesy seems perfectly situated on the Queensway, flanked by established retail development to the west and renewed growth to the east,

this hasn't always been the case. In 1980, when the dealership moved up from the Lakeshore, the neighborhood consisted largely of abandoned industrial land. Since then, Sherway Gardens has expanded, megastores have moved in, and shops, cinemas, and restaurants followed. City planners expect the Queensway will soon be similarly transformed for miles to the east.

Courtesy broke ground for this evolution, and by growing its own business, supporting other area retailers, and raising funds for Etobicoke Hospital, the company has worked to promote the area ever since.

It's All People

Pointing to several employees—all wearing shirts just like his own—Polyschuk says, "It's the people inside the 'uniforms' that make the difference. Our people

have made this a great dealership." For years, most of Courtesy's staff, including its president, have worn the "uniform"—company golf shirts or sweaters in a fresh color every year. The matched casual wear creates a team look for the staff and a more relaxed business environment for customers.

If Courtesy's people are such an asset, the company's stability is its X factor. Turnover is exceptionally low; more than half of Courtesy's employees have been with the company more than 15 years. That degree of continuity builds customer loyalty and makes for satisfying, long-term work relationships. "We really work as a team," says Polyschuk. "We've won GM's Triple Crown many times [an award given to the top 100 dealers in the country], we've never lost a factory sales contest, and last year we earned our ISO 9002 certificate,

which recognizes excellence in business practice by international standards. We were one of the first GM stores in Canada to be certified."

Into the Future

I don't think anyone knows exactly what this business will look like five years down the road," Polyschuk concedes. "But we're certainly not afraid of change—it's what keeps things exciting. We're expanding our presence on the Internet, we're always training bright new people, we have plans to improve our facilities, and my son and daughter, Craig and Stacey, have come into the business with me. I'm really looking forward to the future."

No matter what lies beyond the horizon, it seems safe to assume that Courtesy Chev Olds Ltd. will be part of Toronto's business landscape for a very long time. 🍁

Courtesy's President Don Polyschuk is seen on the dealership patio with his children, Craig and Stacey, who are both active in the business.

Polyschuk with a well-preserved 1961 Corvette, always a favourite with him.

Courtesy's friendly staff is a good part of the reason for the company's high customer satisfaction rating.

Deep Foundations Contractors Inc.

BENEATH TORONTO LIES A LABYRINTH OF UNDERGROUND FACILITIES that support the city. Office towers sit on giant columns of concrete drilled into bedrock. Large vertical shafts are bored through soil and rock to create water and sewage systems. Underground malls, parking garages, and subway lines all require deep

excavation. The work involved in creating these subterranean structures must be precise, carried out by a company with knowledge and experience. Since 1971, Deep Foundations Contractors Inc. has been a premier contractor for such work.

Deep Foundations provides ground support systems during the construction of underground facilities to ensure the stability of soil and buildings. The company installs drilled concrete columns (caissons), underpinning, and piling, as well as performing load testing and marine work. Varying ground and water conditions often require imaginative solutions for excavation support and specialized foundations.

The company was established by David Miller and Bill Lardner, who are both still involved with the business. Peter McDonald and Bill Starke, the two other principals, now operate the business. Collectively, the four

have more than 130 years of experience in excavation support and foundations.

The experience of the team shows on the list of completed projects. History highlights include the Sheppard Avenue subway system, CN Tower, Skydome, Ontario Place, Exhibition Place, Princess Margaret Hospital, The Princess of Wales Theatre, Toronto City Hall, and Highway 407. Deep Foundations has been involved in more than 2,000 projects across Canada and in the Caribbean. Recently, the firm was awarded one of the largest caisson contracts ever in Canada, involving the expansion of Toronto's Lester B. Pearson International Airport.

Leaders in Innovation

From the beginning, Deep Foundations was committed to seeking new and improved ways to provide the products and services needed by

the construction industry. The company's founders developed or introduced a number of innovations to the Toronto construction scene, including soil anchor tie backs for external excavation support, concrete caisson walls for the protection of adjacent building foundations, hydraulic caisson drills, and auger-cast piles.

Dealing with geological anomalies has become a Deep Foundations specialty. Anomalies are almost a certainty with any underground construction, but their location and significance can vary widely. Deep Foundations is structured so that it can respond quickly when unknown anomalies occur. The company has created a team that combines engineers and tradespeople with the experience and resources to deal with unusual geological situations.

Frequently, the challenge of a new project is the source of innovation that becomes a standard solu-

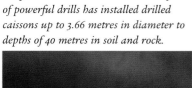

Deep Foundations Contractors Inc.'s fleet of powerful drills has installed drilled caissons up to 3.66 metres in diameter to depths of 40 metres in soil and rock.

An excavation support system and temporary roadway decking allowed traffic to continue over this excavation for the Sheppard Subway System.

tion. The St. Clair River Tunnel was one such story. In late 1993, the tunnel boring machine (TBM) being used in the construction of a new rail tunnel was experiencing problems. The TBM's cutterhead needed to be removed and serviced, but it was located 29 metres below ground in clay described as having the consistency of toothpaste.

Deep Foundations was selected from a number of North American contractors that submitted proposals to create a shaft large enough to bring the 9.5 metre cutterhead to the surface. The firm installed a series of 227 caissons, which required more than seven kilometres of drilling, and created a cylinder of concrete 15 metres in diameter to allow the raising of the cutterhead. It was the first shaft to be successfully constructed in the unusual soil conditions of the area.

For this achievement, Deep Foundations received the Outstanding Project of the Year award from the International Deep Foundations Institute and has since been consulted on similar projects.

Projects like this have cemented Deep Foundations' reputation as a dependable supplier of new alternatives to existing foundation practices.

INVOLVED IN THE INDUSTRY AND COMMUNITY

A number of Deep Foundations' management and staff members hold executive positions with trade and technical associations. The firm is represented on the Board of Directors of the International Association of Drilled Shaft Contractors and on committees of the Canadian Geotechnical Society and the Deep Foundations Institute. Two of the

principals are past presidents of the Ontario Association of Foundation Specialists.

Employees often are asked to provide guest lectures at universities, colleges, and technical associations. The company also is an active participant in the Professional Engineers of Ontario Innovators Program, a collaboration of the professional society and the Ontario Science Centre.

Founding principal Bill Lardner is a past member of the Standing Committee for Structural Design and the National Building Code and the Associated Committee on Geotechnical Research of the National Research Council. He received the Meyerhof Award from the Canadian Geotechnical Society in recognition of his contributions to Canadian science and engineering.

The recipient of several annual safety awards from the International Association of Foundation Drilling, Deep Foundations implemented a comprehensive program in 1993 to identify and correct potentially unsafe practices. A committee, with representation from all departments, meets regularly to review safety practices, procedures, and policies.

Deep Foundations has been a key participant in the construction of many of Toronto's landmarks in the course of building its 30-year history of growth and innovation. 🍁

Deep Foundation's engineers and tradesmen celebrate the completion of the St. Clair Tunnel Rescue Shaft, which was 29-metres deep in unstable soils and the first to be constructed in the area without experiencing a collapse (left).

Deep Foundations installed caissons and shoring associated with CN Tower and Skydome Stadium (right).

CANWEST GLOBAL COMMUNICATIONS CORP.

TELEVISION, RADIO, NEWSPAPERS, AND MAGAZINES—FEW CANADIAN companies can claim to have it all. CanWest Global Communications Corp. is one of Canada's leading international media companies, with operations in six countries worldwide. Since 1974, this upstart company has grown from one small station on the Canadian

prairies to a significant player in the international media scene.

CanWest owns or has substantial interest in six television networks in five countries, specialty television channels in Canada, two radio networks in New Zealand, and more than 130 newspapers and magazines across Canada. CanWest is also a production and distribution company, a Canadian-based television and newspaper marketing company, a new-media company, and an operator of production and postproduction facilities. This company of leading brands is a true convergence conglomerate, uniting the conventional media of print and electronic content with the on-line and interactive technology of the Internet.

While CanWest is a Winnipeg-based corporation, two of the company's flagship operations, Global

Since 1974, CanWest Global Communications Corp. has grown from one small station on the Canadian prairies to a significant player in the international media scene.

Television Network and the *National Post*, are in Toronto and are a crucial part of the city's media landscape.

GLOBAL TELEVISION NETWORK

Started in 1974 as an alternative to the existing mainstream networks, Global Television Network has always had a reputation of being a bit edgier and a lot more fun than Canada's more established networks. The key to Global's early success was its great program schedule that attracted new and younger audiences. Through the 1980s and 1990s, Global became a significant regional broadcaster with a leading prime-time schedule in Toronto and southern Ontario.

Global was the first Canadian station to pick up popular American shows like "Seinfeld," "The Simpsons," and "Friends," as well as broadcasts of NFL football games. Canadian work has always been highlighted

at Global as well. "Traders," a modern take on the drama inherent in a Bay Street brokerage, was one of the most successful Canadian-made shows ever. "Big Sound," a more recent addition to the roster, is a comic take on the recording industry that has attracted an A list of musical guest stars. "Survivor," "The Practice," and "Boston Public" have all been major hits, skewed to a younger audience that the other stations simply had not focussed on.

Global's viewership, cultivated by showing some of the best available Canadian and U.S. productions, has provided the cornerstone to build a network across the country. In July 2000, Global became the third truly national network in Canadian history to be viewable from coast to coast.

Global has long had a reputation for excellent news coverage with some of the most highly respected broadcast journalists in the country, includ-

ing Kevin Newman, Peter Kent, and Beverly Thomson. In 2001, Global launched a new early evening national newscast produced in Vancouver and hosted by Kevin Newman. Global now delivers a complete package of news throughout the dinner hours of 5 to 7 p.m. In addition to its broadcast strength, the company also has a strong on-line presence through the canada.com portal and local Web sites that support Global stations across the country.

NATIONAL POST

Started by the Hollinger Corporation in October 1998, the *National Post* made a big splash on the newspaper scene from day one. Very quickly, the *National Post* virtually tied the other national stalwart, *The Globe and Mail*, for circulation numbers. As of July 2000, CanWest Global had bought 50 percent ownership in Canada's second national newspaper, securing a national print voice to match the company's television reach.

The *National Post* was created from the foundations of a much older Toronto paper, the *Financial Post*, which was Canada's foremost finance tabloid. The current *Post* maintains substantial coverage of business and financial news. The *National Post* quickly attracted some of the leading names in Canadian journalism, including John Fraser, Christie Blatchford, Robert Fulford, Terrance Corcoran, and the late Mordecai Richler.

Similar to Global Television, the *National Post* is distinct from the other offerings in the market. It's literate, but irreverent. It doesn't take itself seriously, yet offers a distinct point of view. Since the revamp of *Saturday Night* magazine and its inclusion in the *Saturday National*

Post, Canadians have found weekend reading much more fun. Now located in the rolling hills of Don Mills just north of the city centre, the *National Post* keeps its finger on the pulse of city, national, and international news.

TORONTO FIREWORKS

The other Toronto presence of the CanWest family is a bit more subtle. Ask members of any of the numerous film productions taking place around the city, and chances are there will be some connection to Fireworks Entertainment. Fireworks is the corporation's development, financing, and production unit. *Caitlin's Way*, a children's live-action drama and a Fireworks production, is one of its most recent success stories. Its Fireworks debut made ratings history in becoming the highest-rated première in the 20-year life span of Nickelodeon.

All in all, Global Television, the *National Post*, and Fireworks Enter-

tainment comprise a mighty triangle of entertainment in the city of Toronto.

CANWEST FOUNDATION

CanWest founder and current Executive Chairman Israel Asper is one of Canada's leading philanthropists, and has instilled in the company a very strong sense of corporate responsibility. The CanWest Foundation was established in 1997 to support causes in the fields of arts and broadcast education. Led by Gail Asper, the foundation supports numerous innovative educational programs, as well as some of the country's most-loved arts festivals.

Like Global Television and the *National Post*, the CanWest Foundation is a part of CanWest Global Communications Corp.'s long-term legacy of commitment to the arts and media for Canadian audiences, readers, and creators to enjoy for a very long time to come.

CanWest owns or has substantial interest in six television networks in five countries, specialty television channels in Canada, two radio networks in New Zealand, and more than 130 newspapers and magazines across Canada.

TIM HORTONS IS ONE OF CANADA'S LEADING NATIONAL FOOD SERVICE chains, serving fresh premium blend coffee, baked goods, and luncheon offerings. Renowned for its quality and great service, Tim Hortons now has more than 1,900 stores from coast to coast in Canada and more than 120 stores in the United States, mainly in

the key markets of Detroit, Buffalo, and Columbus, Ohio.

The founder and namesake of the chain, Tim Horton, was a truly legendary National Hockey League star, playing the vast majority of his 22-year career with the Toronto Maple Leafs. Horton started the chain in Hamilton in 1964, bringing ex-policeman and spirited entrepreneur Ron Joyce on board as the first successful franchisee. With three stores successfully operating by 1967, the two men decided they should become full partners in the business.

As the chain grew, consumer tastes began to change, and so did the menu choices at Tim Hortons stores. In 1976, bite-size treats called Timbits were introduced, and to this day, remain tremendously popular in a wide variety of flavours.

The 1980s saw the Tim Hortons menu expand further to include muffins, cakes, pies, and croissants. By the early 1990s, some 500 stores were open across the nation, with a handful in the United States as well. In 1995, Tim Hortons introduced bagels to its repertoire, and today, the chain has become the top seller of bagels in food service in Canada. The year 2000 saw more groundbreaking events, with the milestone opening of store number 2,000 in downtown Toronto.

Shoppers at Yorkdale Mall can grab lunch or a quick pick-me-up coffee at Tim Hortons.

Tim Hortons is one of Canada's leading national food service chains, serving fresh premium blend coffee, baked goods, and luncheon offerings.

COFFEE, BAKED GOODS, AND MORE

The first Tim Hortons store sold only coffee and doughnuts. But as the times changed, so did consumer tastes, and the Tim Hortons menu expanded accordingly. Joyce, Co-founder and Senior Chairman, says, "We've grown and evolved over the years, which I believe is a big reason for our success to date. Our customers have always depended on the highest quality from Tim Hortons, and we've maintained their trust by always introducing top quality products."

Over the years, Tim Hortons has added hearty soups, "Tim's Own" home-style sandwiches, and chili to the menu. There's some-thing for everyone at any time of the day. But the coffee is what gets people coming back several times a day. Tim Hortons has a chainwide policy that if a pot of coffee isn't served within 20 minutes, it isn't served at all. It's that 20-minute guarantee that ensures customers that they'll always get a consistent cup of great-tasting coffee at Tim Hortons.

STORES THAT FIT IN ANYWHERE

Tim Hortons stores have become a neighbourhood meeting place. From a full standard store with a drive-through, to a mall location like Yorkdale Mall, Tim Hortons offers

its customers a friendly atmosphere and convenient locations. It's a place to talk with friends over a bagel or a doughnut, or just pick up a quick coffee on the way to work. There is even a Tim Hortons kiosk in every terminal of Toronto's Lester B. Pearson International Airport for travellers on the go.

The look of Tim Hortons stores has also evolved over the decades. In downtown Toronto, Tim Hortons 2,000th store is very modern in its design—purple and orange tones, metal chairs—which fits in perfectly in this urban location. Double drive-throughs, which have a window on each side, help to increase efficiency and accessibility, and combo stores with Wendy's offer customers two great concepts under one roof.

TIM HORTON CHILDREN'S FOUNDATION

In 1974, founding partner Tim Horton died in a tragic car accident. Because of Horton's love of children, Joyce and Horton's widow established the Tim Horton Children's Foundation in Horton's memory. Every year, more than 6,000 children from underprivileged families can enjoy an all-expense-paid 10 days of outdoor education and camp fun. The camps are located in Parry Sound, Ontario; Kananaskis, Alberta; Quyon, Quebec; Tatamagouche, Nova Scotia; and the newest—and first U.S.—camp, which opened in Campbellsville, Kentucky, in June 2001. Young people, who are selected from within the communities where Tim Hortons stores operate, are sent to camps outside their own area, making the travel aspect an adventure in itself.

Every year on Camp Day, usually in mid-May, the entire chain contributes all coffee sales from the day, as well as donations from other fundraising activities, to the foundation. The money raised by this fundraiser helps the foundation to continue to create wonderful memories for these deserving children, and also to expand the programs it offers. For example, as part of the foundation's Tracking Program, some children are now able to return to camp for up to five more years, helping them to further develop their self-confidence and leadership skills and to prepare for their future.

It is no wonder that Tim Hortons is frequently the recipient of industry awards. The firm was recently named the Company of the Year for 2000 at the *Foodservice & Hospitality Magazine*'s Pinnacle Awards. "Tim Hortons has come a long way since 1964, but we have always stayed true to our customers through our commitments to community, customer service, and the highest-quality food and beverage products," says Joyce. 🍁

Ron Joyce, who established the Tim Horton Children's Foundation in 1975, meets with some happy kids participating in a camping experience (left).

Kids enjoy making new friends and trying new activities at a Tim Horton Children's Foundation Camp (right).

The chain's milestone 2,000th store is located on the corner of Richmond and Sherbourne streets.

HOMAG CANADA INC.

N THE WOODWORKING INDUSTRY, HOMAG IS ONE OF THE MOST RESPECTED and familiar names in the world. Established in 1975, Homag Canada Inc. is a member of the Homag Group, a global leader in the manufacture of industrial machines for the woodworking and furniture industry. The Homag Group is composed of com-

panies around the world that produce leading-edge products ranging from edge-banding machines to drilling machines, dividing saws, and production plants for the prefabricated housing industry.

More than 40 years ago, Eugene Hornberger and Gerhard Schuler, two brilliant young men involved in the woodworking business, saw an opportunity. They realized that the technology used in binding books could also be used to apply wood strips to the edges of particleboard substraights, solving one of the longest-standing problems in furniture production. Homag invented edge banders that today work near the speed of a printing press. Hornberger and Schuler also realized that larger production facilities needed automated saws, so through Holzma, a member of the Homag Group, horizontal panel dividing saws were born. There are now 12 manufacturing companies in the Homag family, and production facilities can be found in Germany, Spain, Brazil, and China.

Along with this assemblage of leaders in manufacturing are the Homag Group's marketing subsidiaries, experts in consulting and machine engineering whose sole focus is the woodworking industry. A multinational group of 11 sales companies—in Asia, Austria, Canada, Denmark, France, Italy, Japan, Ko-

Homag Canada Inc.'s employees are highly skilled crafts-people whose combined capabilities—both in machine building and in supplying customers in the woodworking industry—create specifically tailored solutions that set them apart from their competitors.

rea, Poland, Russia, and the United Kingdom—facilitates the Homag Group's global presence. Homag's international marketing strategy has representation in virtually every country—from cities in China to Mississauga—making it a tremendous marketing network.

CANADIAN STRATEGY

Canada plays a very important role in the dynamic strategy of Homag and in the panel processing industry as a whole. Canada is a leader in furniture manufacturing, with 80 percent of the furniture made in Canada exported to the United States by name-brand companies like the Global Group, Knoll, Stack-a-Shelf, Talon, South Shore Indus-

tries, Roy & Breton, Lacasse, Palliser, and Smed. Homag Canada has been providing this vibrant industry with the machinery it needs for more than 25 years.

Homag's Canadian organizational headquarters is located in Mississauga, with important subsidiaries in Montreal and Calgary. Each centre has a sales team and service technicians who install and assemble Homag machinery at customers' locations. Homag Canada's staff also provides maintenance programs and repairs as required. A primarily self-sufficient organization, Homag Canada also stocks the appropriate spare parts to back up services.

Homag Canada has enjoyed steady growth since it opened—growth that reflects the expansion of the Canadian woodworking industry. Today, the company has some 40 employees, half of whom are solely dedicated to service.

CUSTOMER SATISFACTION

Homag's customer philosophy is evident everywhere in the organization—from the framed and posted customer satisfaction mission statements to the customized solutions installed and serviced by Homag's staff. The company is clearly dedicated to the needs of the woodworking industry. Homag's

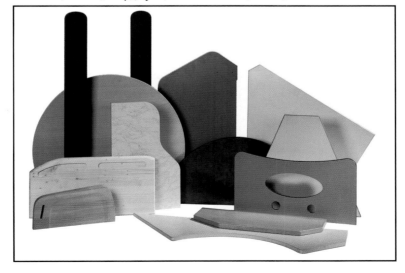

Homag Canada Inc. is a member of the Homag Group, a global leader in the manufacture of industrial machines for the woodworking and furniture industry.

employees are highly skilled crafts-people whose combined capabilities—both in machine building and in supplying customers in the wood-working industry—create specifically tailored solutions that set them apart from their competitors. It is this shared expertise that cultivates good working partnerships.

Due to the complexity of the machines and the demands of the industry, the woodworking industry does more than just buy a machine. It buys an individualized solution and a working Homag partnership.

"We have great rapport with our customers," says Horst Petermann, Managing Director of Homag Canada. "We see ourselves as part-ners with our customers, supply-ing the mechanical portion to their business and enabling them to be successful."

RESEARCH AND EDUCATION

The nature of the woodworking industry demands ongoing improvements in products and service. After all, it was the creation of a radical improvement in wood-working technology that founded Homag in the first place. In order to safeguard the future of its leader-ship in the market, Homag expends approximately 6 percent of its turn-over back into the development of leading-edge technologies.

As one of its latest developments, Homag is now working on the world's first robot-controlled assembly cell. Mechtronics—the integration of mechanics, microelectronics, and information technology—is the ideal condition for new technical innovations at Homag.

In the field of service and commu-nication, Homag is also a pioneer in the field. The company's service and remote diagnostics use modem and satellite technology and the Internet to access technical docu-mentation. Homag is now perfect-ing remote video diagnosis, which will give local customers, wherever they may be, instant access to the global expertise that Homag can supply.

Homag's commitment to research extends to support of educational initiatives as well. Schuler is an honor-ary director of the Rosenheim Insti-tute for Woodworking Technology in Germany. In Canada, Homag

Canada has established ongoing partnerships locally with Conestoga College and the Alberta Institute of Technology. In British Columbia, Homag Canada has been involved in the establishment of the Univer-sity of British Columbia Centre for Advanced Wood Processing, a new college fashioned after the Rosenheim Institute. Since its much anticipated inception, the British Columbia Institute has been graduating new woodworking engineers for several years running.

Ultimately, Homag's extraordinary success can be attributed to what company founders call dynamic strategy. Dynamic strategy involves the ongoing integration of leading manufacturers, as well as the spear-heading of innovations in technol-ogy. Now, and well into the future, the Homag Group and Homag Canada will continue to focus the company's dynamic strategy on its customers, who will, in turn, profit from Homag's expertise and increased service. ♦

Homag's Canadian organizational headquarters is located in Mississauga, with important subsidiaries in Montreal and Calgary.

SOMETIMES A HOTEL CAN PLAY A SIGNIFICANT ROLE IN THE DEVELOPment of a city. In Toronto, the Westin Harbour Castle is one of those hotels. In 1975, when the hotel opened, only a visionary could have predicted how popular the city's harbour front would become and what role the hotel would play in its development. 🍁

The Westin is located on historic Pier 9 where, in 1949, a terrible fire broke out aboard the cruise ship Noronic. Today, relics from the ship and memorials to those who lost their lives are on display at Toronto's waterfront museum. The pier has now become home to the Toronto Island ferry, which transports island residents and picnickers alike to the pretty, treed islands across the lake.

A CASTLE ON THE WATERFRONT

The Westin Harbour Castle and the pier are now at the centre of an ongoing lakefront development and reclamation project that has seen the addition of luxury condominiums, art galleries, an antique market, a theatre, outdoor music festivals, a shopping centre, and a skating rink. This development project continues, as Torontonians and visitors enthusiastically enjoy the beauty of the Lake Ontario

The Westin Harbour Castle is located on historic Pier 9, from which a harbour of lights can be seen on scenic Lake Ontario.

waterfront. It's fair to say that the Westin Harbour Castle was the ground breaker in the evolution of this area.

Not only has the hotel helped to attract attention to the waterfront area, but it has long been associated with several key events and happenings around the city. The Westin Harbour Castle is the official host hotel for the cast and crew of many popular Broadway shows. The hotel also plays host to Maple Leaf Sports and Entertainment Ltd., which manages two of Toronto's wildly popular sports franchises—basketball's Toronto Raptors and hockey's Toronto Maple Leafs.

Due to its pivotal role as a waterfront resident, the Westin Harbour Castle considers cultural responsibility a key part of its corporate citizenship. After all, galleries, theatres, and music festivals bring tourists and Torontonians down to the area on a frequent basis. The Westin is a major

sponsor of one of the city's most spectacular events of the year—The Symphony of Fire, a musical and fireworks extravaganza that attracts professional pyrotechnic artists from around the world.

Over the years, the Westin Harbour Castle has played host to some of the city's most significant special events, including the Juno Awards, the City of Toronto's Millennium New Year's Night, and the annual Sports Celebrities Festival benefiting the Special Olympics. Major gala events for the Toronto Board of Trade, the Multiple Sclerosis Society, Kids Help Phone, the Molson Indy, the Dragon Boat Gala, and Reach for the Rainbow—a children's charity—are also hosted at the Westin. The hotel has been a prime location for a number of political conventions, receptions for heads of state and foreign dignitaries, and conferences for Canada's leading industries.

A Harbour of Luxury

The Harbour Castle is part of Westin's family of 110 upscale hotels and resorts in 23 countries—owned/managed facilities, joint ventures, and franchises. Westin itself is part of an international accommodation network owned by Starwood Hotels and Resorts Worldwide. As part of this globally renowned network, the Westin Harbour Castle boasts many of the latest developments in service and luxury.

Westin set the industry standard for outstanding hospitality as the first hotel chain in North America. Among Westin's innovations are 24-hour room service, the guest credit card, computerized reservations, and a family plan allowing children under 18 to stay free with their parents.

Business Travel News has rated Westin as the best U.S. upscale hotel chain for an unprecedented four years, with the UK's *Business Travel World* magazine rating the chain as the best business hotel in both the United States and Canada. In its first-ever survey of hotel guest satisfaction, J.D. Power & Associates ranked Westin highest in upscale guest satisfaction. Such awards, which are among the many that Westin has received, plus executive stability and a lower-than-average employee turnover rate, are all keys to why Westin continues to enjoy the brand loyalty it has built over the years.

Toronto's Westin Harbour Castle has individual charms of its own and is held to the high standards of quality, elegance, and service that guests have come to expect from Westin hotels around the world. Guests can really see the best of Toronto's spectacular lake and city views, and the hotel also boasts renowned restaurants, as well as exceptional meeting and conference facilities.

The Harbour Castle is the only hotel in Toronto with a connecting conference centre. The corporate convention facility, appropriate for a wide variety of business meetings and events, is one of the finest in the city, with more than 70,000 square feet of function space.

With its unsurpassed combination of luxury, amenities, history, and spectacular views of Toronto, the Westin Harbour Castle truly offers all that one could want from a hotel. ◆

Luxury awaits Westin Harbour Castle guests in the hotel's elegant main lobby (left).

The hotel's Executive Suite is just one of the recent hotel renovations (right).

The Westin Harbour Castle's Regatta Room is suitable for any VIP function.

T WAS IN 1978 THAT MICHAEL MACMILLAN AND HIS PARTNERS OPENED Atlantis Films. From a tiny office in an old house on Church Street in Toronto, they made documentaries for $20,000; each partner drew a salary of $100 a week. The bank was not happy. 🍁 Cut to 1984. Atlantis won an Academy Award for best short drama. The bank was happy.

Cut to 2001. MacMillan, now chairman and CEO, and his partners at Alliance Atlantis Communications Inc. are in another office off Church Street, this time a tower with the company's name on top. They are in charge of Canada's largest integrated film and television company, with more than $750 million in annual revenues, more than 800 employees working from offices in seven production centres around the world, and major interests in film and television production and distribution, including broadcasting.

When thinking about what happened, one can call it Canadian chutzpah. In a country with only 10 percent of North America's population, and a world where entertainment giants roam the earth with brands and revenues many times those of Alliance Atlantis, this Toronto-born company has chalked up an enviable record—by anyone's beanstalk.

Alliance Atlantis now exports its television productions to more than 250 countries around the world, from "Due South" in Azerbaijan, to "Traders" in Germany and France, to "C.S.I.: Crime Scene Investigation," seen in the United States, as well as in Canada. In fact, more than 80 percent of the company's revenues come from outside Canada—a large factor in making Canada the second-largest exporter of television programming in the world.

"C.S.I.: Crime Scene Investigation," coproduced by Alliance Atlantis Communications Inc. for CBS, was the highest-rated new television series of the 2000-2001 season, starring (back, from left) Paul Guilfoyle, Jorja Fox, Gary Dourdan, George Eads, (front) Marg Helgenberger, and William Peterson.

In 2001 alone, the Alliance Atlantis series "C.S.I.: Crime Scene Investigation" was the highest-rated new dramatic series on CBS' entire prime-time schedule. Also in 2001, in its broadcast group, Alliance Atlantis launched U8TV.com, Canada's first Internet channel, which features the entertaining reality of eight young people living together—not always in blissful harmony—and broadcast on the Internet 24 hours a day, seven days a week, with a highlights package shown Monday to Friday on the company's popular Life Network. In other words, by being able to produce, distribute, and broadcast its own programming, Alliance Atlantis is able to achieve the benefits of integration, while

spreading its risks in an industry that is better known for taking them.

The company has been producing and distributing film and television programs so successfully, and for so long, that it now has a library of some 14,000 hours of programming, with the long-term revenue stream implied by that number.

HOW IT ALL WORKS

Alliance Atlantis is successful because the television group mainly creates and distributes TV series, mini-series, and movies-of-the-week. And through the company's two specialized production divisions, it also focusses on documentary and non-fiction programs, via AAC FACT™, and on children's live-action and animated series, via AAC KIDS™. The firm sells the rights to all of these programs to Canadian and international networks, as well as to its own networks.

It's no coincidence, then, that Alliance Atlantis' broadcast group has interests in 18 specialty TV networks that have become name brands for millions of Canadians to turn to—Showcase, Life Network, Home & Garden Television (HGTV Canada), History Television, Series +, Historia, Headline Sports—The Score, and Food Network Canada—as well as U8TV. That's only the tip of the beanstalk. In September 2001, Alliance

Produced by Alliance Atlantis for TNT Network, "Nuremberg" was one of cable television's highest rated mini-series starring (from left) Alec Baldwin, Jill Hennessy, and Christopher Plummer.

JAN THIJS

JOHNNIE EISEN

Atlantis launched several new digital channels, including Discovery Health Channel, National Geographic Canada, BBC Canada, BBC Kids, and Independent Film Channel Canada.

On the motion picture side, Alliance Atlantis is by far the largest distributor of motion pictures in Canada. In 2000 alone, the company's motion picture group released more than 80 movies and made six of its own, which were distributed worldwide. These upscale, director-driven pictures included the Academy Award-nominated *The Sweet Hereafter,* the

Golden Globe-nominated *Sunshine,* and the critically acclaimed *Felicia's Journey.*

The company's Cinevillage, operated as a full-production studio for Alliance Atlantis and other companies since 1985, continues to chalk up busy years. Little wonder: while Toronto is often called Hollywood North because of the number of U.S. film and television productions that are shot and edited in the area, a big part of that volume comes from Alliance Atlantis' productions that are shooting in the company's own

backyard. In 2000 alone, some $200 million was spent by Alliance Atlantis in Toronto on productions, creating some 2,500 jobs to fuel the region's economy.

GIVING BACK

Alliance Atlantis Communications Inc. also gives back to the Toronto area in other ways: the company has committed more than $4 million to supporting excellence in Canada's fast-growing entertainment industry, with $1.8 million in start-up dollars for a new centre of learning—the Canadian Broadcast and Production and Executive Training Program. Presented jointly by the Banff Television Foundation, the Banff Centre for Management, and Alliance Atlantis, the program focusses on developing entrepreneurial leadership and management skills to equip senior Canadians in television and new media for the challenges of a global marketplace—the very qualities that Alliance Atlantis Communications Inc. itself so richly embodies.

"It's not clear who will win from the convergence revolution going on all around us," says MacMillan. "What is clear is that the companies who have the ability to both produce and distribute their own content in as many ways as consumers want will prevail. That is our strategy, and as new technologies multiply the new forms of distribution, we'll be ready for the future, no matter what it throws our way." 🍁

Ralph Fiennes stars in Istvan Szabo's Sunshine, *an Alliance Atlantis motion picture (left).*

Ian Holm stars in Atom Egoyan's The Sweet Hereafter, *an Alliance Atlantis motion picture (right).*

Emeril Lagasse hosts "Emeril Live" on Food Network Canada, one of Alliance Atlantis' 18 analog specialty television networks.

ADP Canada

NE OUT OF EVERY FIVE CANADIANS EMPLOYED IN THE PRIVATE sector receives a paycheque from ADP Canada. ADP Canada is one of the country's leading providers of employer services, with a comprehensive range of payroll, human resources management systems, time and labour management, and tax filing services.

From the regular weekly paycheque of a private nanny to the compensation plan for a major Canadian bank, ADP Canada relieves Canadian employers from the time-consuming task of administration.

ADP Canada is a wholly owned subsidiary of Automatic Data Processing Inc., one of the world's largest providers of transaction processing. Its roots in Canada reach back for more than 20 years, since the company began to offer its world-class service in a Canadian context. While ADP Canada originated in Toronto in 1979, the company now has 22 locations across the country and in all the major markets.

The principles behind ADP's service are the same in both Canada and the United States. "Few people are payroll experts, so what we do is help employers run their businesses—helping them focus on their own growth and what they do best," explains Rod Dobson, President, ADP Canada. "We're here to provide complete and comprehensive employer solutions from recruitment to retirement."

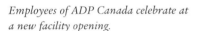

ADP Canada President Rod Dobson

Employees of ADP Canada celebrate at a new facility opening.

WORLD-CLASS SERVICE

World-class service is much more than just the company mission—it is the ADP way of life. Everyone, from receptionists to salespeople to administrators, understands that the level of service that ADP can deliver will keep it miles ahead of the competition. The principles of world-class service are posted throughout ADP's offices to remind and inspire all employees to give their very best to ADP clients.

To ADP Canada, world-class service means meeting precise expectations, fulfilling commitments to clients, routinely exceeding client expectations, always anticipating client needs, and ultimately helping clients improve their businesses. For ADP, constant and energetic commitment to service has resulted in phenomenal growth.

DAILY GROWTH

ADP has been enjoying significant growth in the recent past in particular, as companies return their focus to core competencies. ADP Canada serviced clients with only 400 employees before 1997; by 2000, business demand had caused the number of employees to increase to more than 1,600.

The reason ADP Canada has grown so quickly is a simple one: the company is always looking for ways to improve products and services available to customers. One recent innovation is people@work™. An ADP-hosted Human Resources Management solution that is fully Web-operational, people@work offers a wealth of functionality available right from a client's Internet browser. While ADP Canada will continue to invest in these and other Internet-based solutions, it will continue to be a matter of choice

Dobson and employees of ADP Canada.

for its clients. ADP will offer its clients flexibility and choice through both client/server and Web-based platforms.

ADP had the opportunity to process the payroll for an entire territory when the Government of Nunavut turned to ADP for payroll and human resources solutions. ADP offered quick turnaround and innovative processes for the far-northern community, and ADP Canada is already saving money for the government.

ADP's commitment to improving service often results in new technologies. For example, e-TIME is a software package that automates time and attendance tracking—employees simply swipe their ID badges through an electronic time clock, and the software calculates total pay. Another useful innovation is iNETPay, a free, confidential calculator for net pay. Much of the implementation of these tools happens at ADP's new, state-of-the-art data centre in Mississauga, which boasts a mainframe open system and high-capacity storage subsystem.

EMPLOYER OF CHOICE

ADP Canada is focussed on being the employer of choice for Canadians. "Our employees are the mainstay of our business," explains Dobson. "They understand the importance of the role they play—getting paycheques to people, and being accurate and timely about business. I speak for myself, as well as for all of our employ-

ees, when I say that we are very proud to work for such a financially sound and progressive company."

The company's efforts to be an employer of choice centre on a few core areas that provide opportunity, career development, recognition, and an environment that encourages meaningful contributions. ADP Canada provides career progression programs, a tuition reimbursement program, and career opportunity programs, including intranet posting. The company frequently and visibly recognizes special efforts and success stories, as well as provides extra

services in peak work periods.

Contributions are encouraged at ADP Canada through a culture of teamwork and collaboration between departments and regions. The company is committed to helping each employee find the right work/life balance through education tools, resource and referral programs, and expanded flexible work arrangements.

"We have a good number of people who have been here since our Canadian inception more than 20 years ago," says Dobson. "That speaks volumes about how much we value our employees." 🍁

The grand opening of a new facility in Mississauga, Ontario

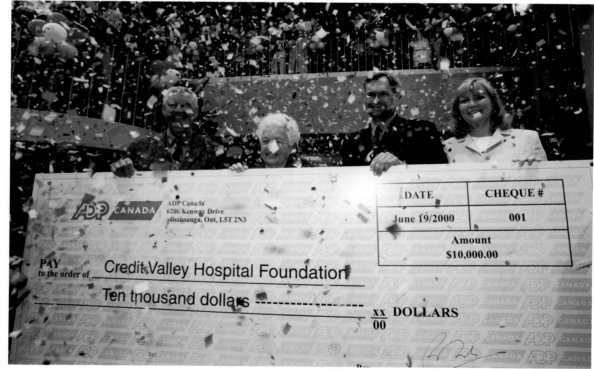

REX PAK LIMITED, FOUNDED IN 1974, IS CANADA'S LEADING FOOD blending and packaging comanufacturer. Rex Pak is an owner-managed company now into its second generation. Louis Sabatini, cofounder and current president of the company, is the brains behind Rex Pak's packaging machines. From his early tinkering

in the 1970s to his in-demand expertise in the 21st century, Sabatini still spends time every day with the packaging machinery that makes the business run. Steve Napier, Senior Partner and General Manager, has been with Rex Pak since 1978. John Medeiros, Partner and Plant Manager, has overlooked production since 1977.

When asked about the company name, Sabatini says, "Rex means king." With almost 30 years of experience, Rex Pak has indeed become the king of packagers in Canada. From sugar substitutes to jelly powders, hot chocolates to soup mix, Rex Pak can create specialized packaging for virtually any dry food product.

Over the last several years, blending and packaging needs have become much more complex. Gourmet soups, for example, require an enormous range of items—from dried spices and vegetables to special seasonings—and all must be blended perfectly to exacting standards. Pizza can now be assembled from a box that contains tomato sauce, crust, and cheese—all separately packaged. Rex Pak has become the only Torontonian manufacturer capable of meeting a huge range of the dry food industry's demands.

FLEXIBILITY IN A CHANGING MARKETPLACE

Rex Pak's customers are household names in food; in fact, some of the firm's customers have been using Rex Pak's services for more than 25 years. The reason for customer loyalty is simple: great service, great pricing, and, above all, flexibility. With more than 30 computerized production lines and four blending rooms, Rex Pak can handle any large production run, yet still be flexible enough for smaller customers.

Flexibility is critical in the food blending and packaging industry, as quick changeovers and smaller production runs are normal in the Canadian market. Rex Pak has helped launch many new products, becoming a leading resource for new product development.

STATE-OF-THE-ART PRODUCTION FACILITY

The first thing that strikes a visitor to the gleaming, blue Rex Pak building is its crisp cleanliness. Employees in white lab coats and hygienic caps work in a humidity-controlled, 90,000-square-foot complex that resembles a high-tech scientific laboratory. However, the experts here create the latest in packaged food.

In its new facility near Highway 401, Rex Pak has built a plant that meets the toughest industry standards. Agriculture Canada has granted Rex Pak its highest possible licence, a Canadian Food Inspection Agency licence to operate a registered meat/dairy establishment. Rex Pak continually upgrades its equipment, which run at very high speeds and is considered among the most efficient of its kind in North America.

A state-of-the-art facility must be staffed by equally skilled people. More than 90 percent of the firm's some 100 employees have been involved with the company for five years or more. In addition, profit sharing for employees encourages a collegial and productive atmosphere. "Our people are the best," Sabatini says . "Each of them is an expert at his or her job."

As packaging needs become more complex through the years, Rex Pak Limited will be able to meet and adhere to industry standards, providing the best in quality foods to consumers.

Since 1974, Rex Pak Limited has been meeting industry standards to fulfill packaging needs.

The Rex Pak management team consists of (seated) Louis Sabatini, (standing from left) Devin Sabatini, John Medeiros, Steve Napier, and Denise Sabatini-Fuina

INDUSTRY   INTEGRITY

INTELLIGENCE

▲ © JUDY NISENHOLT

TORONTO

1975
2001

1975	Homag Canada Inc.
1975	The Westin Harbour Castle
1978	Alliance Atlantis Communications, Inc.
1979	ADP Canada
1981	Teknion Corporation
1982	ADC Software Systems Canada Ltd.
1983	NLnovalink
1985	Trebor Personnel Inc.
1988	Delfour Corporation
1989	Airport Group Canada Inc.
1990	AllCanada Express Limited
1990	Holiday Inn On King
1991	Biovail Corporation
1991	Teranet Inc.
1993	The Alliance Personnel Group Inc.
1996	Adecco Employment Services Limited
1996	Greater Toronto Airports Authority
1999	Ontario Power Generation
1999	The Scarborough Hospital

TEKNION CORPORATION

EKNION CORPORATION IS A REMARKABLE CANADIAN SUCCESS STORY in the contract furniture industry. Headquartered in Toronto, the company is one of the fastest-growing and most-feared competitors in the business, with sales increasing at a compound annual growth rate of 40 percent since 1995. Teknion—a market leader in Canada—

is an international designer, manufacturer, and marketer of office systems and related products, including storage and filing, seating, casegoods, tables, and ergonomic furniture. Teknion employs more than 4,900 people worldwide, and operates 26 manufacturing facilities that, together with showrooms, corporate headquarters, and sales offices, total more than 2.5 million square feet. The company's products are sold in more than 50 countries through a network of more than 400 authorized dealers.

Teknion grew out of the Global Group of Companies in response to the vast increase in business technologies in the late 1970s and early 1980s—particularly the personal computer and fax machine. Teknion was formed in 1981 to create high-performance workplace solutions.

RESPONSIVE

Teknion has created a legacy of innovation, responding both to specific customer needs and to general changes in the work environment. The company's products are both aesthetic and adaptable. Teknion's Transit, T/O/S, Leverage, and Expansion office furniture systems address varied workplace needs. The firm's sleek Ability line includes mobile furniture, which can be reconfigured as needed. Its Altos architectural wall system provides visual and acoustic privacy, as well as fully flexible office space, and can be relocated. Recently, Teknion introduced xm, an office furniture collection that combines classic, elegant design; maximum integration of workplace technology; and the ultimate in user control.

Responding quickly to customer needs has been key to Teknion's success, as has the company's ability to customize existing—or to create new—products tailored to the individual needs of clients. As a result of this responsiveness, Teknion has built an enviable client roster of some of the leading companies in the world.

"Our entrepreneurial culture breeds a high degree of flexibility and responsiveness to the needs of our customers," says David Feldberg, President and CEO. "In many ways and in many areas of our operations, we conduct business with a personal touch—and that represents a very real competitive edge for Teknion."

AGILE

In the current environment, responsiveness must combine with agility and speed. Teknion is a large international company that works like a small company in terms of its ability to change. The firm's product strat-

Transit Free-standing office furniture offers attractive, cost-effective solutions for small offices and growing businesses.

Altos is a relocatable, full-height architectural wall system from Teknion.

egy is developed by a steering team comprised of individuals from all the key areas of the company that unite in an energetic process to guide the direction of product development.

"Our responsiveness and timely solutions—basically, our agility—have meant that we can introduce new lines in an exceptionally short time frame," says Feldberg. "Everyone from design, engineering, manufacturing, sales, and marketing works in concert."

HUMAN

Understanding how people sit and move over the course of a workday is the foundation of Teknion's success. Each product has the user in mind exclusively. "The spaces people work in and the tools they use act as a catalyst for achieving both individual and organizational success," explains Feldberg. "Simple tools can help to create the intangibles of inspiration, commitment, and community."

Teknion's human-centered phi-losophy guides its business in terms of both design and the culture the company has endeavored to create for those who contribute their time and talent. Teknion is committed to investing in its people, facilities, and technology to maintain the firm's leadership and momentum.

"Our human capital is perhaps the single most important factor in our success as a company," says Feldberg.

CLEVER

As an innovative, design-driven company, Teknion recognizes the importance of forging close relationships with such partners as designers and architects. The rewards of these partnerships are reflected in the design of Teknion's marketing materials, offices, and showrooms, and perhaps even more so in the company's corporate headquarters in Toronto. The new building, created by Moriyama & Teshima in conjunction with Rice Brydone, features Teknion's products in a Living Lab that illustrates the wide array of workplace responses Teknion provides.

Teknion continually wins awards for design innovation. The company has received more than 50 prestigious industry design awards. Teknion won the National Post Design Exchange Gold Award, and is a frequent award winner at NeoCon, North America's largest interior design and facilities management show, held in Chicago each year. The firm has won awards from the prestigious *International Design Magazine*—including recognition in the publication's I.D. Forty, a list of North America's most design-driven companies—and has also earned the Design of the Decade Award from the Industrial Designers Society of America, as well as the Best of Canada prize awarded by *Canadian Interiors* magazine.

Today, as it has since its founding, Teknion Corporation is creating business tools that will change the boundaries of work and the workplace of the future. 🍁

T/O/S Architectural Elements create impact with style, including metal and glazed options (left).

Gemini is an elegant wood casegoods collection with a classic contemporary feel by Halcon, a Teknion company (right).

Teknion is an international designer, manufacturer, and marketer of office systems and related products, including the Advocate seating collection.

ADC SOFTWARE SYSTEMS CANADA LTD.

LOCATED IN THE HEART OF TORONTO'S MARKHAM TECHNOLOGY DISTRICT, ADC Software Systems Canada Ltd. has been an integral part of this growing neighbourhood since 1982. Formerly Saville Systems, a world innovator of convergent billing systems, ADC Software Systems has considerable experience in the burgeoning telecom-

munications billing software industry.

From its modest beginnings, the company has quickly grown to become a premier member of the industry, complete with worldwide offices and global customers. Global offices include locations in western Canada, Ireland, England, the United States, and Australia.

ADC Software Systems is a division of ADC Telecommunications, a US$3.2 billion global supplier of systems and solutions for telecommunications, cable television, broadcast, wireless, and enterprise networks. Founded as an electrical products company by Ralph Alison, an inventive Minneapolis engineer, in 1935, ADC's products now perform critical functions for broadband networks throughout the world. ADC's customers include some of the world's best-known telephone companies, cable television operators, and Internet/data service providers.

SINGULARIT.E

Focus on the customer has driven ADC Software Systems to global success. Staying one step ahead of the competition has always characterized ADC, and it is that approach that the company passes on to customers. The firm understands how to help its customers cultivate loyalty, and creates its services and solutions accordingly. ADC's Singularit.e is a suite of comprehensive operations support system software products and consulting services, a talented team of people, and a broad service base for integrated communications providers to achieve that goal.

The theme of Singularit.e is one point, one vision, and one view: one point of contact for end-to-end automation; one vision of an integrated team; and one view—a real-time, Web-enabled view of customer, service, and network information. ADC's extensive catalogue of solutions and services enables service providers to customize bundles of services and discount pricing structures in accordance with their needs.

DYNAMIC WORKPLACE

Due to the excitement and phenomenal growth in the industry, ADC attracts some of the best and brightest people to its employ. "Our success is built on the foundation of intellectual capital," says Minda Sherman, Vice President of Human Resources. "So that's where we make our greatest investment." Employees are offered constant opportunities to invest in their skills, as well as to explore greater opportunities in software development solutions and in building broadband infrastructure.

A global company with offices in some of the most interesting places in the world, ADC offers extraordinary possibilities for growth in either customer-related or software-

intensive careers. In the late 1990s, the company invested in a state-of-the art work facility designed specifically for ADC's operations and staff. This new building is equipped with high-end facilities and considerable outdoor space in order to provide an exceptional work environment for ADC's employees.

More than $1 billion worldwide is invested daily in communications networks. With that number in mind, ADC Software Systems Canada Ltd. has a bright future ahead. On the cutting edge of technology needs, demands, and services, and with customer demand growing, ADC is well positioned to meet the challenges of an increasingly technological world. 🍁

Located in the heart of Toronto's Markham technology district, ADC Software Systems Canada Ltd. is a division of ADC Telecommunications, a US$3.2 billion global supplier of systems and solutions for telecommunications, cable television, broadcast, wireless, and enterprise networks.

KNOWING THAT THE PERSONAL TOUCH IS CRUCIAL IN THE PERSONNEL business, Trebor Personnel Inc. (TPI) President Bob Bryce has focussed on this element since the company's inception. Bryce and his wife, Brenda, founded Trebor in 1985 to provide quality industrial and transportation personnel to southern Ontario.

Since then, the business has grown steadily. "We've been obsessed with customer service and satisfaction from day one," says Bryce.

Trebor provides wholly integrated employee services solutions for its industrial and manufacturing customers. Not only does the company recruit and interview employees, but it also offers an extensive roster of employee services. Trebor can provide its customers with complete payroll setup, weekly payroll drop-off, on-site supervision, aptitude testing, and health and safety training. Staff members are available 24 hours a day, seven days a week.

From Kitchener to Belleville, Trebor has the waterfront covered with nine regional offices. Offices are also located in Mississauga, Burlington, and Brampton, as well as several Toronto locations. While each individual office is focussed on catering to the local economy with local talent and local expertise, every Trebor office maintains high standards that customers rely on. Trebor is an ISO 9002 registered company—honouring rigorous standards in procedure and policy. ISO 9002 registration ensures that Trebor delivers complete consistency in service across its network of offices.

Trebor Personnel has a high profile in the Greater Toronto area, allowing it to attract some of the most interesting and productive customers in the region, but also some of the best employees.

Trebor Personnel Inc. President Bob Bryce and his wife, Brenda, have focussed on keeping a personal touch in the personnel business since founding the company in 1985.

SERVICES TO MEET EVERY PERSONNEL NEED

The foundation of Trebor's business has historically been temporary labour, industrial staffing, and driver services—a vast range of skill and experience levels. Every year, Trebor sends some 5,000 people to work. Among these workers are packers; dock workers; forklift operators; and class AZ, DZ, and G drivers for the pharmaceutical, food, warehousing, pulp and paper, plumbing, mechanical, waste and recycling, and promotional packaging industries.

Trebor also offers a temporary-to-permanent program, whereby clients can evaluate a potential employee while on the job and make final hiring decisions without the usual costs and risks associated with new hires.

Due to customer demand, Trebor has recently expanded to office and technical staff. Clients were so pleased with the comprehensive staffing services that Trebor provides that they began to insist on an expansion in types of employees. Now customers can enjoy the services of qualified, experienced office staff. Data entry professionals, bookkeepers, customer service specialists, purchasing clerks, accounts payable and accounts receivable clerks, secretaries, and receptionists are all available on a temporary, permanent, or contract basis through Trebor.

Communication and professionalism have been key to Trebor's success so far, and Bryce brings his personal approach and open communications style to each and every client. This personal approach also inspires Trebor employees to be thorough, professional, and ethical. "We will continue to focus on our strengths," says Bryce. "The quality of our people and the work that they do ultimately create value for our clients."

STYLIZED VICTORY GESTURES, SHOUTS OF GLEE, AND GROANS OF DEFEAT regularly resonate after hours through the halls of NLnovalink in Mississauga. Foosball is taken seriously at the company; the tables were introduced as a way of combating potential carpal tunnel problems associated with extensive computer usage. The results have

been phenomenal: the foosball talent and playful competitive spirit have created heroes and friendships amongst both office and factory workers alike.

NLnovalink management is very proud of today's staff. Diverse and international backgrounds blend to create NLnovalink's team of highly experienced core members and new recruits. Training and developing people, extending opportunity, and, in return, receiving loyalty and hard work is the basic formula behind NLnovalink's success.

Along with this familial-like sense of teamwork, NLnovalink has been able to flourish due to the economic and social climates of Toronto and Mississauga. "Toronto," explains the co-founding team of Maria and Tony Vander Park, "is a city where innovative ideas and hard work can find positive encouragement. It is a democratic locale where some of Canada's largest companies were willing to open their doors to small upstarts." Indeed, two of NLnovalink's first customers were Bell Canada and the

Royal Bank. Started in a 2-bedroom Port Credit apartment and now housed in its own 80,000-square-foot manufacturing plant at the 401 and Mississauga Road, NLnovalink has remained a Mississauga company for its entire 18 years of existence.

A PRODUCT AND A PROCESS™

NLnovalink, a contract furniture company with multiple patents around the world, has pioneered the flexible and very reliable Product and Process™ concept. An advanced modular method, it employs a standardized spine system, the product, and a CAD/CAM production capability, the process, to provide furniture solutions for many diverse applications in technology intensive work environments.

The Product and Process concept allows the company to focus on its customer's needs. The in-house CAD/CAM design and manufacturing capability lets NLnovalink produce custom components that match the user's equipment exactly. The combined power of the Product and

Process method will thus result in a correct installation on day one and a sustainable asset thereafter.

Comprised of Fortune 500 companies, NLnovalink's customers are institutions, corporations and government offices. NLnovalink installations can be found around the world including Dubai, Mumbai (formerly Bombay), Singapore, Tokyo, London, Madrid, Buenos Aires, Caracas, Sydney, Amsterdam, Seoul, Houston, Vancouver, New York, and Toronto.

NLNOVALINK: A PROGRESSION

Incorporated in 1983, NLnovalink began as a mechanical design and procurement company in a Port Credit, Mississauga apartment. The first product was an expandable chassis system for a Bell Canada special assembly telephone. This telephone program led directly to the financial trading room business, with clients such as The Royal Bank, Toronto-Dominion Bank, and Citibank.

NLnovalink, riding a 35 percent annual growth rate, has moved every

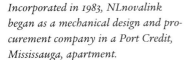

Incorporated in 1983, NLnovalink began as a mechanical design and procurement company in a Port Credit, Mississauga, apartment.

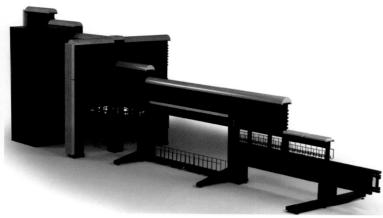

five years when its size would double or even triple. Today, NLnovalink is housed in its new headquarters and production complex. The state-of-the-art facility is a symbol of the company's success and the embodiment of its values. More than a trophy-type icon to reinforce NLnovalink's presence, the facility gives the entire staff a sense of increased worth. The grounds of the campus are immaculately landscaped. Inside NLnovalink's dramatic foyer, one finds a new age, high-tech look complemented with many traditional, high-quality materials. Slate floors, patterned and sculpted carpet sections, open ceilings, suspended drywall bulkheads, and accentuating cherry millwork: everywhere you look, there is a sense of generous space.

The NLnovalink showroom displays a wide variety of the technology intensive workstation applications: trading desks, network operations centre consoles, 911/Emergency dispatch consoles, network server equipment fixtures, heavy-duty workstations, and a large security-

monitoring console (all using the same core spine structure). The NLnovalink operations floor is the image of a trading floor with high ceilings, low, open furniture for excellent sight lines, indirect lighting, and lots of accessible cable management.

The production plant is fully climate controlled, with air conditioning, air filtration, and dust removal systems. The company is highly conscious of the environment; the plant has a zero-emissions powder paint line, which meets ISO 14000 environmental criteria. The plant makes extensive use of computer numeric control machines, not only for their production efficiency, but also for worker safety as well. Ontario Workmen's Compensation actually pays NLnovalink rebates.

Toronto, with its people, its corporations and institutions, its political and economic environment, has allowed a small company to achieve significant successes both at home and afar. NLnovalink in turn is proud to promote these qualities around the world. 🍁

NLnovalink installations can be found around the world, with its customers including major corporations, institutions, and governments.

DELFOUR CORPORATION

THE INTERNET HAS RADICALLY CHANGED THE WORLD OF LOGISTICS, and Delfour Corporation, a world leader in the development of information technology systems for the third-party and contract logistics industry, is at the forefront of that change. Delfour's advanced information products and applications, which improve the

effectiveness of warehousing processes with unique applications and solutions, have made the firm a pioneer in the industry.

The young company's growth pace has been considerable. Delfour was formed by a group of professionals who understood warehousing and logistics. Consulting and software-related services were provided to North American warehousing organizations before the company was founded in 1988 in the heart of the high-tech district just north of Toronto. Today, the company has a global presence in eight countries.

With its state-of-the-art facility headquartered in Markham, Delfour Corporation is expanding globally.

THE E-LOGISTICS REVOLUTION

The evolution of e-logistics and the trend toward logistics outsourcing in recent years have in combination completely changed how the logistics industry works. Technology has allowed for considerably higher and more consistent abilities for organizations in need of logistics services. And companies are much more likely to rely on the expertise of logistics specialists rather than handle their logistics operations internally. Client Richard A. Reynolds of AmeriFreeze explains, "By using cutting-edge inventory control technology, Delfour has optimized our

customer inventory throughout. This has reduced costs to our cold storage clientele, and has dramatically improved our overall warehouse productivity and performance, allowing us to pass on streamlined cost reductions to our customers."

The use of relational database management systems and the recent move to Java technology have enabled Delfour to maintain its leading role in the production and implementation of logistics systems. Proprietary software meticulously tracks the progress of shipped products and manages the receipt of inventory. Clients can now track manufactured

goods from plant departure, through transit, to arrival at distribution centers, as well as shipment to multiple points. Many other software companies have already adopted the unique features developed by Delfour to improve their own applications.

A wide range of companies in many industries now benefit from Delfour's leading-edge technology. The firm's third-party logistics clients include many of the world's most prominent shippers. The market continues to grow rapidly as companies worldwide seek to outsource their logistics challenges.

Although some of these clients are not third-party logistics providers, they are still able to utilize the multiclient features within such Delfour products as WarehouseLogic. Delfour logistics solutions are driven by customers' processes and requirements, an approach that distinguishes the company from its competitors. "We focus our attention on listening to and understanding our clients' needs," says Joe Couto, President of Delfour Corporation. Solutions have been designed to meet the specific needs and procedures of each organization, and can handle multiple facilities and multiple customers simultaneously, in contrast to competitors' products that typically require a different system for each facility.

Technical support is offered to Delfour clients 24 hours a day, seven days a week.

Breadth of Service

To stay ahead of this quickly evolving industry, Delfour offers a wider range of specialized logistics solutions that fit every client. "Our first customer installed on a Delfour system had very complex requirements," says Larry Willet of California Distribution. "The support we received from the entire Delfour staff to meet our very aggressive targets was outstanding."

Delfour offers consulting to its clients in the areas of warehouse and distribution operations, as well as warehouse management systems and implementation. The company also offers a comprehensive set of instructor-based courses to meet the specific needs of its clients.

In the logistics industry, research and new products are critical. New, Web-enabled applications are always being developed by the Delfour team. In August 2000, Delfour launched the e-Vista product, which offers the clients of third-party logistics providers Web access to their information.

This Web-based system has drill-down capabilities for easy use, and customers can use a simple view or print the information using their local printer.

Delfour is now expanding its role in supply-chain management by integrating Delfour applications with supply chain management applications that manage the entire life of a product—from inception to arrival at the customer's door. Says Couto, "Looking to the future, we will ensure a deeper involvement in the flow for the best possible business performance."

Delfour also enjoys high demand for information systems from other sectors. World leaders in high technology, telecommunications, food, hazardous goods, automotive components, pulp and paper, household goods, and heavy equipment now store and ship their products through many of Delfour's systems.

As a result of growing customer demand, the company has expanded globally from its headquarters in Markham, and now has offices and employees in Argentina, Brazil, the United Kingdom, and the United States. Delfour has also extended its reach to Chile and Mexico. Falabella, a partner with Home Depot, incorporates Delfour systems to operate Chile's largest department store. In Mexico, Transportation Maritima Mexicana (TMM), one of the country's largest logistics providers, now employs Delfour's technology to operate the port of Acapulco.

The concept of a tailorable configuration tool has continued to be at the core of Delfour Corporation's product evolution. Advanced technology has been the cornerstone of this company's growth and expertise, and will continue to provide the fuel for the logistics industry well into the future. 🍁

Whether it's third party logistics, ambient (dry) or controlled (cold) storage, Delfour Corporation applies logic and technology to solve the warehouse puzzle.

T'S NOT SOMETHING THAT OCCURS TO MOST PEOPLE RACING TO CATCH a flight, but a well-run terminal can make the difference between a pleasant journey and a nightmarish one. Toronto Pearson International Airport's Terminal 3, managed by Airport Group Canada Inc., offers the setting and services that make it one of the best-run terminals in the world. From top-quality dining choices to the well-lit vaulted ceiling in the main terminal building, and from the innovative design that allows arriving and departing passengers to use fully separated floors to the connected Sheraton Hotel, Terminal 3 stands out from the crowd.

Airport Group Canada manages and maintains all aspects of the Pearson Terminal 3 complex, including the 1,000-foot-long grand hall; 100,000 square feet of retail space; 29 gates; 41 elevators; 31 escalators; 16 powered walkways; and a baggage system that handles some 2,500 bags an hour—all in a building of some 1.3 million square feet. The facility currently handles more than 9 million passengers.

Airport Group Canada is also responsible for other aspects of Pearson, including the management of public and employee parking at all three terminals—translating to literally millions of cars every year. The group is also responsible for the shuttle buses linking the three terminals with the parking lots.

Frank Walsh, General Manager, explains the success of the operation: "Our biggest supporters are our tenants. The service we provide for them is the foundation of our business. We have excellent relationships here in Toronto—it's a great partnership that makes for a great airport."

GLOBAL REACH, LOCAL KNOWLEDGE

Airport Group Canada is part of TBI, a worldwide player in airport management. TBI originated in England in 1995 as a property-based business, but saw an opportunity shortly thereafter to help turn airports into financial success stories. Since then, TBI has grown and now operates across four continents in 10 countries at more than 30 airports where they manage or own airport operations and provide a comprehensive range of services at each location. With this growth has come a world of expertise in airport management. More than 2,600 staff worldwide work in all aspects of airport management in both large and small regional and urban facilities. The new direction in the airport industry is clearly one of mutually advantageous partnerships that marry TBI's financing, management expertise, and business acumen in airport operation with local input and knowledge.

No airport is too big or too small to take advantage of TBI's expertise. A company committed to working with communities to help turn their airports into viable, income-generating operations, TBI's focus is on providing the management and expertise that can develop airports and the airport property business.

The pace of growth in the airport industry is relentless. With travelers and cargo needs increasing every year, TBI—along with Airport Group Canada Inc.—is positioned to help airports throughout the world become more profitable.🍁

Airport Group Canada Inc. manages Terminal 3 at Toronto Pearson International Airport, which offers the setting and services that make it one of the best-run terminals in the world.

THE ALLIANCE PERSONNEL GROUP INC. IS ONE OF CANADA'S FORE-most providers of logistics personnel, warehouse facilities, operations management, and certified logistics training. Through The Alliance Personnel Group, companies are able to count on receiving the most comprehensive and responsive staffing,

warehousing, and training services available.

As a national company with locations in Calgary, Kingston, Medicine Hat, Mississauga, Montreal, Oakville, Saskatoon, Vancouver, and Winnipeg, The Alliance Group can provide services to companies across the country. The Alliance Group has approximately 1,400 employees providing service for major companies, including Nortel, Imperial Oil, Haliburton Energy Services, and Praxair Canada.

Alliance's two founding partners have been in business together for some 20 years. Jon Cooper and Tom McNeil have exceptional expertise in warehousing and trucking, respectively. Though this incarnation of the company has only been around since 1993, under the leadership of this dynamic duo, The Alliance Personnel Group has seen a double-digit increase in sales each year since its inception.

STAFFING:
THE PEOPLE PEOPLE

The employees of The Alliance Group form the foundation of the company. Alliance's staffing services are in demand in a huge variety of industries from automotive to warehousing. Employees are experts in several key areas: commercial and

specialized transportation, clerical and administrative services, warehouse management, and payroll administration. The Alliance Personnel Group provides customized and detailed solutions to individual client employment needs.

Cooper, one of the founding partners, explains how he sees the role of employees: "No one goes into business to be an employer, yet it is one of the most important things you can do in business. We go the extra mile for our employees, and it makes a difference—they do a wonderful job."

LOGISTICS:
THE TIMELY DIVISION

The Alliance Group has built a strong reputation in logistics, specifically with complete warehouse and distribution services. "Our experience and capabilities in warehousing are comprehensive," says Cooper. "We can provide the space, book the staff, and run the warehousing facility as a single, seamless service." The outsourcing of warehousing to state-of-the-art facilities and dedicated warehouse specialists can be an ideal business solution.

Included in the logistics division of the company are its transportation services. Alliance can provide a staff of drivers, as well as the trucks

CRAIG MINIELLY MPA/AURA

and dispatch services, for virtually every transportation need. The Alliance Group sets stringent criteria for safety and customer service to help ensure that every delivery arrives on time.

COMPREHENSIVE TRAINING:
THE FOCUS

What sets The Alliance Group apart from others in the industry is its commitment to training. Specialized training programs have been designed to build a staff with more depth. For example, the company offers complete classroom and behind-the-wheel driver instruction that is recognized for its very high standards.

Safety is, of course, a crucial part of the training experience—going well beyond the learning centres—and is an integral part of the culture of The Alliance Personnel Group. The firm is an active member of the Alberta Safe- ty Council, Ontario Trucking Association, and Warehousing Education and Research Council.

"Our focus is on safety, customer service, and systems, with ongoing improvement in these three areas all the time," explains Cooper. "Ultimately, to be responsive to our clients is our focus as a company."

Providing its services across the country, The Alliance Personnel Group Inc. helps companies receive the most comprehensive and responsive staffing, warehousing, and training services available.

HIGH ABOVE THE TRADITIONAL INFRASTRUCTURE OF THE CITY IS a business that keeps Toronto moving. AllCanada Express Limited is a major Canadian provider of aircraft, crews, and flight services to the air courier and freight industry. All through the night, AllCanada Express serves the world from its Canadian home, delivering the critical supplies needed to keep the economy moving.

AllCanada Express acts as the east-west backbone of courier operations like UPS and Royal Cargo. AllCanada operates nightly western flights connecting Vancouver, Calgary, Winnipeg, Hamilton, and Mirabel Airport, Montreal, as well as eastern runs covering Hamilton, Halifax, Moncton, and St. John's. From points across Canada, cargo is also collected and flown south of the border to the major U.S. cargo hubs.

An AllCanada Express Limited Boeing 727-200 cargo plane on approach.

TWO GUYS, ONE IDEA

All that founding partners John MacKenzie and Murray Lantz had was the idea to create a new Canadian air cargo company, a few decades of experience, and a prior reputation for fairness and a focus on on-time performance. Their key advantage was an abiding passion for the business and the often underestimated power of engaging

AllCanada's record of more than 99 percent on-time service is exemplary.

GARY TAHIR

personalities. It was easy to see how their expertise and experience engendered instant confidence in those early days.

MacKenzie and Lantz had identified an important niche. "We knew that the change in manufacturing from whenever to just-in-time was going to significantly increase the need for air cargo," says MacKenzie. But, as one can imagine, starting an airline from scratch required considerable capital investment for even one cargo plane. MacKenzie and Lantz put together some self- and family-generated seed funding, and began their business by renting an aircraft on a pay-as-you-fly basis.

In September 1992, MacKenzie and Lantz got their first break: a Christmas contract with a major international courier, UPS. AllCanada Express was up and flying. By August 1994, the company had established an exceptional level of performance in on-time delivery. This led to a contract with BAX Global, a major opportunity that would require a Boeing 727, a much larger aircraft than MacKenzie and Lantz owned at the time.

The company needed a 727—and fast. In short order, a suitable aircraft was found stored in the southwestern U.S. desert, but it was hardly ready for flight. Courier companies, and indeed the entire airline industry, have substantial and exacting standards for aircraft. Two months

later, and just in time for the beginning of the contract, AllCanada's first large aircraft was ready.

Now, AllCanada operates 11 Boeing 727s, the largest fleet of Boeing 727-200 series cargo aircraft in Canada. Since then, business for AllCanada has been smooth flying. Strong and steady growth has occurred as the industry AllCanada serves continues to expand, and the company's reputation continues to impress. AllCanada now has several major cross-Canada contracts and third-party maintenance contracts. Employing some 75 pilots and 60 maintenance engineers, AllCanada enjoys a diverse customer base with half its business covering Canada and the other half crossing the border.

Since its relatively recent inception, the company has enjoyed some exotic cargo, such as the U.S. Equestrian Team's horses—whose transportation specifications and in-flight meal requirements are quite particular. The bread and butter of the AllCanada business, however, are the documents, parts, and components that feed the industries that drive the economy: companies like Celistica and Nortel, and the entire auto industry. "We've done well by finding the right niche in freight, staying focussed, and doing what we do best," says MacKenzie.

Recently, the company has expanded to Hamilton, opening a major cargo maintenance and

▲ GARY TAHIR

Engineers routinely meet all AllCanada Express aircraft.

administrative facility at the John C. Munro Hamilton International Airport. Less than an hour's drive from downtown Toronto, Hamilton is becoming a new cargo hub for the Golden Horseshoe and central Canada. AllCanada has built a 50,000-square-foot hangar and a 30,000-square-foot office space— all needed for the company's expanding business.

ACE FLYERS

From the Roots leather flying jackets—custom made with the AllCanada Express logo—to the very best in maintenance technology, AllCanada treats its employees with the highest regard. Lantz, Vice President of Operations, explains, "Our pilots and engineers are the heart and soul of our business. They have very challenging jobs, so we make it a priority to provide them with the best possible tools. The result is we have a very low turnover and an incredible team of dedicated professionals."

The company has built its reputation on great customer service, a tough taskmaster when customer service is rated on a performance only as good as last night's flight. In that context, AllCanada's record of more than 99 percent on-time service is exemplary. This has been achieved,

in no small part, by the company's emphasis on maintenance practices and maintenance performance—a focus that has been so successful that AllCanada now has contracts to provide its high standards of maintenance to other aircraft fleets.

AllCanada is very involved in the industry as a whole. The company is a member of the Airport Transport Association of Canada, and MacKenzie is chairman of the orga-

nization's cargo committee. The company sees its role in the industry as continually raising the bar on the professional delivery of air cargo service. "We continue to be guided by our founding principles: safety, on-time performance, and strong commitment to maintenance," says MacKenzie. AllCanada Express Limited is a responsible freight airline dedicated to safe operations and reliable customer service. 🍁

▲ GARY TAHIR

OLIDAY INN IS ONE OF THOSE COMFORTING NAMES THAT BECKONS travellers around the world. Although the hotel chain's name is familiar and most customers have an idea of what kind of accommodation to expect, the Holiday Inn On King in the heart of downtown Toronto exceeds those expectations. 🍁 In look and

services offered, the Holiday Inn On King is far from typical. The hotel itself is located in the heart of the city's thriving entertainment district. Not far from the towers of power on Bay Street, Holiday Inn stands out among the quaint, low-rise shops; clubs; and restaurants that neighbour it. Cleverly tiered, the hotel softens its sharp angles with smooth curves, and marries the urban tower with the beachside resort. Even the green-blue fenestration that enhances the building's whiteness helps give it a kind of Mediterranean presence in Toronto.

The 40,000-square-foot Meeting Convention Conference Centre optimizes three easily accessible levels in the hotel. The centre provides 28 highly flexible break-out rooms, and boasts a 10,000-square-foot, state-of-the-art conference centre for business and banquet functions. The centre's convention level, located on the mezzanine floor, comprises two ballrooms of 10,000 square feet each, providing a total of more than 20,000 square feet of contemporary convention,

Holiday Inn On King provides residents and travellers an opportunity to take advantage of all that Toronto has to offer, and to do so in an enjoyable environment.

banquet, and trade show facilities that can comfortably accommodate up to 1,100 people. Floors two through eight offer modern office spaces, which are leased out to various cor-

porate clients, with the second floor holding 11 meeting rooms. The ninth floor and above houses 425 spacious, modern rooms—every one with a view of the city, as well as high-speed modem access, data ports, Nintendo games, and other amenities such as irons, ironing boards, coffee makers, and movies.

GREAT LOCATION AND SWISS HOSPITALITY

One of the keys to the hotel's top performance is its strategic location. At the core of Canada's largest and most dynamic business centre and in the heart of Toronto's entertainment district, the hotel takes full advantage of its great central location to emphasize its business and pleasure persona.

Guests can find live theatre, a mega-movie palace, concert venues, sports arenas, and more than 150 dance clubs and restaurants only steps away. Equally close are many of the spectacular landmarks and attractions that draw millions of people to the city every year, such as the CN Tower, Skydome, Air Canada Centre, Roy Thomson Hall, and Royal Alexandra and Princess of Wales theatres. The

trendy Queen Street shopping district is also nearby, as is the Metro Toronto Convention Centre and National Trade Centre. For business travellers who are accustomed to returning to their rooms after a hard day's work, the Holiday Inn On King offers excitement and activity right outside the front door.

The Holiday Inn On King is supported by a Swiss business group headed by Juerg Sommer. "We wanted to bring Swiss hospitality to Toronto and make this Holiday Inn a popular downtown destination—for both vacationers and corporate travellers," Sommer says.

Almost as soon as it opened, the Holiday Inn On King became an award-winning hotel, fully booked every weekend. The hotel has won the Best Romantic Getaway Package from Toronto's *NOW Magazine*, and is one of the busiest Holiday Inns in the world during the week, catering to hundreds of business travellers and numerous corporate events. The Holiday Inn On King has garnered three Torchbearer Awards, the top award for Holiday Inn and a rare honor among the thousands of Holiday Inns worldwide.

THE KING COMMUNITY

The hotel, however, would not be the success it is without its loyal staff, many of whom have been there since it opened. The Swiss owners' management philosophy is simple: give management the flexibility and support to try new ideas; encourage employees to grow in their jobs at the hotel; give all employees the incentive to make their hotel a success; and be part of the community.

The result is a motivated staff who initiated many of the cutting-edge programs that make this Holiday Inn stand out. Among the ideas developed at the Holiday Inn On King that have become the gold standard of service at Holiday Inns worldwide are the 60 Second Meeting Planner, an easy way to plan successful meetings and small conferences in under a minute; STAYassured, a special program for women travellers; and Show Stoppers, a series of entertainment packages that include tickets to the hottest shows in town.

The Holiday Inn On King is also an active player in the community, and serves as a member of the Met-

ropolitan Toronto Convention and Visitors Bureau and as a founding member of the Entertainment District Association. The hotel's staff members also reflect the diversity of one of Canada's largest and most multinational cities. They are able to welcome guests in 40 different languages.

For hotel manager Marlin Keranen, it is important not only that staff members feel they can play a significant role at the hotel, but also that they can play a significant role in the community. One project that has touched Toronto's heart is the King Clowns, a performing troupe of clowns—composed of staff from the hotel—that began as a team-building exercise for senior management. The

group had so much fun clowning around and making each other laugh that they decided they wanted to bring the same delight to those less fortunate. The troupe now gives regular performances in hospitals, at special events, and on behalf of a variety of charitable organizations in and around Toronto. "It's become a great way of giving back to the community that helped make us successful," says Keranen.

With a worldly and dedicated staff, and a reputation for quality and service, the Holiday Inn On King provides residents and travellers an opportunity to take advantage of all that Toronto has to offer—and to do so in an enjoyable environment.🍁

One of the keys to the hotel's top performance is its strategic location, and the hotel takes full advantage of its great central location to emphasize its business and pleasure persona.

BIOVAIL CORPORATION

AN INTERNATIONAL, FULLY INTEGRATED PHARMACEUTICAL COMPANY with special capabilities in the development, manufacture, sale, and marketing of branded pharmaceutical products, Biovail Corporation builds on its strengths in the development of drugs utilizing advanced controlled-release and FlashDose

technologies. Making medicines better is Biovail's mission, and its success in this area has made the company a major player in the international pharmaceutical industry since its founding in 1991. Medical science has produced an extraordinary number of innovative medications for the treatment of serious illnesses and diseases, and Biovail focusses on making many of these medications more effective through the company's world-leading expertise in the science of controlled-release drug delivery technology.

The advantages of daily controlled-release medicines over standard immediate-release multiple-dose drugs are many. Individuals suffering from chronic conditions like heart disease, depression, and arthritis often have to take two or more doses of their medication daily. For these people, the advantages of controlled-release once-daily dosing can make a substantial difference in their quality of life.

Research has shown that a medication is more effective if it is absorbed in the system in an even, controlled manner, instead of all at once. When a drug is absorbed steadily over time, the side effects are minimized while the overall effectiveness can be substantially increased. In addition, people are also more likely to take their medication if the dosing regime is simplified and the side effects are reduced. Biovail is Canada's leading company focussed on the develop-

Making medicines better is the mission of Biovail Corporation, and its success in this area has made the company a major player in the international pharmaceutical industry.

ment of controlled-release drug delivery technology.

Biovail's scientists have developed a number of proprietary controlled-release technologies. These technologies—alone or in combination—can be applied to a wide variety of medications to produce a superior final product. In 1999, Biovail increased its scientific expertise in this area through the acquisition of Fuisz Technologies Limited, a respected drug development company located in Virginia and Ireland. In 2000, Biovail acquired DJ Pharmaceuticals Incorporated, a U.S. sales and marketing organization, giving the company access to the most lucrative pharmaceutical market in the world. Also in 2000, Biovail acquired marketing rights to one of the world's

leading controlled-release cardiovascular medications, Cardizem CD.

A CANADIAN SUCCESS STORY

Eugene Melnyk, founder and Chairman of the Board at Biovail, started his first business, the medical publishing company Trimel Corporation, when he was just 23. This business achieved a rapid success. Before long, Trimel was publishing more than 40 titles, and was a force to be reckoned with in the Canadian medical publishing industry.

In 1989, Melnyk sold his publishing assets to the Thompson Corporation and acquired Biovail SA, a small, innovative Swiss medical research firm specializing in controlled-release drug delivery. Soon, the new

Biovail Corporation had constructed a state-of-the-art manufacturing facility near Steinbach, Manitoba, and a plant in Carolina, Puerto Rico.

A Canadian marketing division, Crystaal, was soon created and also achieved significant success. Crystaal's portfolio includes products developed and manufactured by Biovail, as well as branded products licensed from international drug-manufacturing companies.

Biovail is now an international, full-service pharmaceutical company engaged in the formulation, clinical testing, registration, manufacture, distribution, and promotion of pharmaceutical products, most of which utilize advanced drug delivery technologies.

"We are now positioned as one of the world's leading controlled-release companies," says Melnyk. "We have a wide range of products, an international scope—our products are marketing in more than 55 countries—and six core technologies that have the potential of being applied to virtually all oral medicines."

The company's corporate head office is located in Toronto, with modern manufacturing facilities in Steinbach, as well as in Dorado and Carolina, Puerto Rico; research and development operations in Dublin, Ireland, and Chantilly, Virginia; and the new U.S. sales and marketing head office in Raleigh.

Also located in Toronto is Biovail Contract Research, a stand-alone Biovail division that provides full-service clinical research and laboratory testing for international pharmaceutical companies, as well as for Biovail. The 44,000-square-foot facility includes a bioanalytical laboratory and two separate live-in biocenter clinics where studies are performed. The research center has the advantage of a very large regional population to draw on, state-of-the-art technology, and leading experts in the industry.

A PLAN FOR THE FUTURE

Biovail's growth in a relatively short period of time has been spectacular, driven by a corporate strategy that has been both aggressive and conservative. As Melnyk explains, "Our growth has been strategic. Our original revenue streams were diversified: Crystaal, the Contract Research Division, and sales of our generic portfolio. This has been enhanced by the ongoing growth of existing and new branded product lines, including products found by Biovail Ventures, which has a mandate to invest in early-stage technology and product development, and the expansion of our sales force in the U.S. These developments have served us well, and we now have direct access to a huge new market with a complete, fully integrated North American business. Whatever happens, we're ready."

Growth does not happen without a dedicated, professional work force, and Biovail is able to attract the best in North American pharmaceutical talent by being a good employer. The company offers a stock option program, a hands-on work environment, and a corporate culture of openness and innovation. The company's flexibility and entrepreneurial spirit encourage employees and allow Biovail the ability to move quickly to develop new products and respond to opportunities in the market.

Biovail Corporation is now well positioned not only to develop controlled-release medications, but also to market and distribute these superior pharmaceutical medications throughout North America. Biovail will continue to launch new and better pharmaceutical products, either internally developed or acquired, through its significant North American sales and marketing organization. Biovail is making medicines better. 🍁

Biovail Corporation is now well positioned not only to develop controlled-release medications, but also to market and distribute these superior pharmaceutical medications throughout North America.

Teranet Inc.

ERANET INC. IS TRULY A CANADIAN E-COMMERCE SUCCESS STORY. Founded in 1991, Teranet uses its expertise to help public and private sector organizations make their data and services both secure and accessible in the electronic market. ❦ As a result of this focussed strategy, Teranet enjoyed a more than 600 percent

growth rate from 1995 to 2000, an exceptional accomplishment. The company is particularly proud to be among the Deloitte & Touche Canadian Technology Fast 50 for 2000, which honoured Teranet as one of Canada's fastest-growing high-tech companies. Teranet was also recognized as one of the fastest-growing technology companies in North America by the Deloitte & Touche Technology Fast 500.

Teranet was formed as a ground-breaking public/private partnership between the Ontario Ministry of Consumer and Business Services and a group of private-sector investors. The company's mandate was to automate Ontario's 200-year-old, paper-based Land Registry System, one of the world's largest automation and conversion projects. A key outcome of that initial mandate was the development of the e-reg™ software, resulting in the world's first paperless Land Registration System and the birth of a dynamic e-commerce company.

Ground-Breaking E-Government

Teranet automated the Ontario Land Registration System and helped to create the POLARIS® database of document images, title indexes, and maps. The Teraview® gateway allows customers to search and view records and documents on title, submit documents for registration on title, conduct writs of execution searches,

and purchase title insurance—all on-line.

Using its experience and understanding of the needs of the legal profession, Teranet has created the BAR-eX™ portal, a joint venture with the Law Society of Upper Canada and the Lawyers' Professional Indemnity Company. An on-line community for lawyers, the BAR-eX Web site provides a broad range of valuable services and information of interest to the legal community. The site also offers discussion forums, chat rooms, and bulletin boards—an ideal vehicle for active participation by the legal professional.

Teranet is expanding by marketing its e-commerce expertise. The e-comUnity™ Access program enables governments to upgrade their elec-

tronic service delivery quickly and efficiently. The Unity™ framework is a complete e-commerce solution designed to assist governments and data-rich organizations create their own electronic service delivery solutions. Unity is specifically designed with the needs of government in mind, helping the government to better connect with its citizens and interact with commercial entities with which it conducts business.

Due to its enduring relationship with various levels of government, Teranet understands the pressures being faced by governments—such as the need for increased technological efficiency with limited expenditure. One of the greatest advantages of the Unity framework is its inherent flexibility. Unity allows governments to continue ongoing supplier relationships and to focus their efforts on the quality of the service to stakeholders, rather than being distracted by the complexity of the technology itself.

Evolving Partnerships

The relationship that Teranet has with the Ontario Government expanded within and beyond the Ministry of Consumer and Business Services to the Ministry of the Attorney General. At the same time, the company has expanded its expertise successfully into the realm of private

For 200 years, land registration transactions in Ontario involved mountains of paper; today, the process can be done in a fraction of the time, without a single sheet of paper, by using Teranet Inc.'s e-reg™ software—all electronic, paperless, and secure.

Aris Kaplanis, Teranet President and CEO (far right), holds a strategy meeting with members of Teranet's executive team.

WWW.DAVIDEURISNO.COM

With a wide range of products, services, and programs, Teranet is an e-commerce company that provides solutions for the business-to-government and business-to-business marketplace.

sector alliances. Teranet now partners with dozens of government and private sector organizations.

Teranet has created an award-winning group of products that service a very diverse client group. The success of Teranet is in part a direct result of its strong network of strategic alliances. The company's approach to partnering is fundamental to the Teranet philosophy: shared risk, shared reward. Teranet is as committed as its partners are to the success of its e-commerce strategies. A Teranet business partner explains the quality of partnering with Teranet: "Trust makes it work."

CONNECTING COMMUNITY

Trust and partnership play important roles within Teranet as well. A company's culture can be measured in many ways, but one of the most telling statistics is employee turnover. With a staff of some 850 employees, Teranet has a less than 5 percent turnover rate, almost unheard of in a competitive high-tech environment. Teranet's employees are highly valued, and opportunities for growth abound. Aris Kaplanis, President and CEO, gives full credit for the company's success to its employees and customers: "We are successful because we have a great staff, as well as outstanding customers. Our employees are an incredibly committed, energetic, and focussed group. They drive our innovations and our solutions."

Reflecting the energy and commitment of its people, Teranet supports a number of charitable causes with a focus on children and young people. Key recipients of Teranet support are Reach for the Rainbow, which helps disabled youth and children; Raptors Foundation, which works with economically disadvantaged young people; and Operation Springboard, an organization with programs to help youth at risk or in conflict with the law. "It's an important part of our culture to help young people," says Kaplanis. "We're committed to creating opportunities and helping to level the playing field."

In just a few short years, Teranet has made its mark in e-government and e-commerce business services. The future success of Teranet will be based on its ability to help organizations and businesses create flexible, dynamic solutions that give secure access to their services and information. From land ownership transactions to e-commerce and e-government, Teranet Inc. remains a dynamic industry leader. 🍁

Teranet Data Centre staff check the operation of a Teraview® "failover" server. Data centre services reliably ensure that all mission critical systems, networks, servers, and desktops are kept operational 24 hours a day, seven days a week.

◆ ©JONATHAN POSTAL / TOWERY PUBLISHING, INC.

ADECCO EMPLOYMENT SERVICES LIMITED

B Y EVERY MEASURE, THE 1996 MERGER OF ADIA SA OF SWITZERLAND and Ecco SA of France to create Adecco Employment Services Limited marked the formation of a world leader in employment services. Adecco's principal business is providing personnel services to companies and industry worldwide by sourcing

temporary personnel, placing permanent employees, training and testing temporary and permanent employees, outsourcing, and providing outplacement services. Adecco provides these services to businesses located throughout Asia, Europe, Latin America, and North America.

Market conditions indicate why employment services are one of the fastest-growing industries in the world. When Adecco was formed, the firm's goal was to define a new model of personnel services company that would be able to anticipate, and cope with, the radical changes taking place in society, in the economy, and in employment on a global scale.

Today, Adecco is clearly a world leader in the employment industry, with some 4,500 offices in 60 countries throughout the world and the highest market share in eight of the top 13 markets worldwide—Australia, Canada, France, Scandinavia, Spain, Switzerland, the United Kingdom, and the United States. Adecco boasts a worldwide network of more than 28,000 permanent employees who staff more than 200,000 companies with up to 600,000 associates on any given day.

Adecco Employment Services Limited's principal business is providing personnel services to companies and industry worldwide.

ADECCO IN CANADA

Canada currently enjoys a booming job market. Employment levels haven't been so high since the 1960s. New work opportunities exist in almost every industry, sector, and market. Every year in Canada, Adecco is the point of entry and re-entry for thousands of workers to this dynamic new economy.

Branch offices, specialized by skills and industry, are located in every major Canadian city. Every day more than 600 Adecco colleagues facilitate the work of between 12,000 and 15,000 temporary/contract employees.

In the Greater Toronto area alone, Adecco has more than a dozen neighborhood offices placing Adecco associates in a vast array of industries, including office administration, customer service, finance and account-

ing; management; telemarketing; information technology; and light industrial. Companies seeking staff for positions in these and other areas rely on Adecco for consistently well-trained and dedicated personnel.

DELIVERING THE BEST QUALITY PEOPLE TO CLIENTS

By carefully screening all applicants, Adecco is able to create mutually satisfying and rewarding relationships between businesses and the staff the company places with them. Adecco's recruiting personnel are highly trained professionals who possess a comprehensive set of the staffing industry's recruiting strategies,

tactics, and tools. In Toronto, Adecco—as well as using traditional recruitment tactics—finds associates by sponsoring recruiting events with, and posting job listings at, local trade schools, colleges, and universities, as well as at community and retail centres.

Fitting the right workers to the right jobs is accomplished through Xpert®, Adecco's state-of-the-art, computerized screening system. Xpert® evaluates such factors as motivation, work attitude, and labour environment preferences, as well as skills.

Newer to the scene is Adecco's interactive Canadian Web site, www.adecco.ca. Here, job seekers can search for available jobs by specialty and geographical location,

The Adecco survey also identified the huge role part-time, freelance, temporary, and internship employment plays in the search for the perfect job. When asked if they had ever made the transition from temporary to full-time employment in the same company, 29 percent of Canadians said they had.

In the sellers market that is the current Toronto employment scene, the companies at which Adecco associates are placed on assignment are hiring more and more associates for full-time positions. Adecco sees this as a win-win-win situation. Clients get an employee whose suitability for the job they have already tested; associates know they are joining a company they like; and Adecco places an ambassador with the company.

In Toronto, as around the world, Adecco temporary associates play a vital role in the production of countless goods and services that make the city great. From factory floor to engineering lab to executive suite, Adecco delivers the human resources powering today's flexible work force.

Today, Adecco is clearly a world leader in the employment industry, with some 4,500 offices in 60 countries throughout the world and the highest market share in eight of the top 13 markets worldwide.

enabling a work force from Canada and around the world to take the first steps in finding employment in Toronto and elsewhere.

CREATING REWARDING EMPLOYMENT

Adecco provides meaningful career growth and lifestyle benefits for its associate employees—those people who are placed on assignments ranging from short-term, temporary positions to permanent careers. Through one-on-one interviews and Xpert®, Adecco ensures that associates receive placements that dovetail with their personal career aspirations.

Attention to individual needs underscores Adecco's respectful approach to associates' desires. Flex work is one of Adecco's innovative ways of meeting this commitment. Increasing numbers of people are opting for temporary and part-time employment out of a desire to gain greater control over their time and lives. By creating flexible work solutions, Adecco is leading the way

in offering people greater control over, and responsibility for, their career paths.

A GLOBAL COMPANY WITH LOCAL FOCUS

By successfully balancing a global perspective with attention to the unique nature of each market's business needs, Adecco rises above other personnel services companies. In Canada, Adecco conducts the New World at Work survey to keep up to date on employment trends in every province in which the company operates.

Adecco's most recent survey confirmed that flexible staffing, including the use of freelancers, part-timers, and an on-demand work force is now universally recognized as a core component in Canadian business strategy. In response, 23 percent of Canadians surveyed predicted they will be moving to part-time jobs in the next five years, and 20 percent stated that they intended to start freelancing in that time frame.

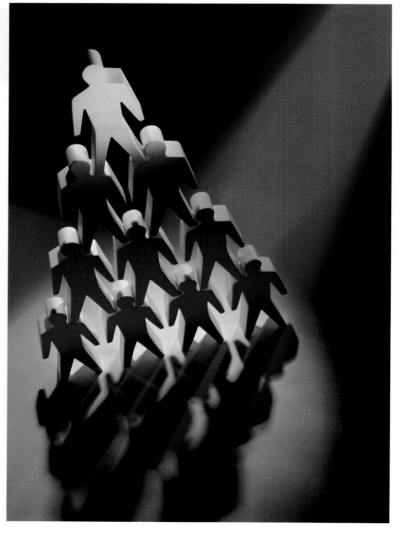

ATE ONE AUGUST DAY IN 1938, LOCAL RESIDENTS AND DIGNITARIES watched as an American Airlines DC-3 made the first official landing at Malton Airport, just outside Toronto. The airport consisted of two hard-surface runways and a grass landing strip, and used a converted farmhouse for its terminal. Malton became

The Greater Toronto Airport Authority (GTAA) was created to operate and develop Pearson Airport to meet the current and future demands for air services for the Greater Toronto Area and surrounding communities.

Toronto International Airport in 1959, and was renamed in 1984 to honour Lester Pearson, Canada's 14th prime minister.

Six decades after that first flight, Toronto Pearson International Airport is Canada's busiest airport and ranks 25th in the world. Currently the airport handles almost 30 million passengers annually, with that number expected to rise to an estimated 50 million passengers per year by 2020. The Greater Toronto Airports Authority (GTAA) has responded to the challenge of this impressive growth with a 20-year master plan that will redevelop the airport from the inside out. "It is not a matter of 'if we build it, they will come,'" says GTAA President Louis A. Turpen. "We're building this airport because they are coming."

FROM FARMERS' FIELDS TO A NORTH AMERICAN HUB

Driving this growth is Pearson Airport's development into a major international gateway to rival the facilities of the Kennedy and O'Hare airports. New, long-range jets—

combined with Toronto's proximity to the United States with preborder clearance capabilities—give Pearson Airport the strategic advantages necessary to make it the northeastern gateway to North America for both passengers and cargo. Approximately 360,000 metric tons of freight now flow through the airport per year, a

figure that will rise to approximately 675,000 metric tons by 2020. As the population of the Greater Toronto Area increases in the coming decades, air freight will become a vital aspect of the local infrastructure, and those needs will be served by a major infield cargo development.

GTAA was created to operate

GTAA has responded to the impressive growth of the Lester B. Pearson International Airport, which currently handles almost 30 million passengers annually, with that number expected to rise to an estimated 50 million passengers per year by 2020.

and develop Pearson Airport to meet the current and future demands for air services for the Greater Toronto Area and surrounding communities. Incorporated as a not-for-profit, non-share capital corporation in 1993, GTAA assumed management, operation, and maintenance of Pearson Airport in 1996. In 1999, the extensive redevelopment program at Pearson Airport began to take shape. The 20-year redevelopment master plan is designed to provide a platform for the airline industry to expand services over time.

Pearson Airport will continue to function normally throughout the redevelopment process. In effect, this will mean building virtually a new airport on an existing facility. Even the demolition of the old terminals will cause no significant disruptions in service.

A VISIONARY REDEVELOPMENT

GTAA was created in the context of the National Airports Policy, which required that it be run as a private—but community oriented— corporation. The GTAA Board includes nominees from each surrounding regional municipality and from the provincial and federal governments. As a result, the plans of the GTAA take into account the needs and concerns of the surrounding communities, and seek to share opportunities with them. "Consulting and reaching agreements with neighbouring communities and all levels of government is a cornerstone in everything we do," says Turpen.

The 20-year plan has three major

stages. Between 2000 and 2003 the first portion of the new terminal will be built. GTAA's architectural partners have designed the new terminal to ensure passengers enjoy a journey that is both pleasant and easy to navigate. Reminiscent of aviation itself, wide-open spaces will combine with natural light flooding in from above to create a sense of ease. The new terminal will replace current Terminals 1 and 2, and will have a gross floor area equivalent to 55 football fields. Covered pedestrian bridges will lead to a new, eight-storey parking garage—Canada's largest parking structure—which will ultimately allow for 12,600 parking spaces. Ceilings will be higher than typical parking garages to accommodate SUVs with roof racks. Airside improvements will include the construction of a dual taxiway, a fifth runway, and a sixth runway.

Over the course of the redevelopment, transportation in and out of the airport will be improved. The section of Highway 409 west of Highway 427 has been purchased by GTAA and is being realigned to lead directly into the new terminal, with loop roads connecting it to Terminal 3. Highway 427 will continue to have a direct access to the airport.

An automated people-mover will connect the new terminal to Terminal 3. Between 2005 and 2010, Terminal 2 will be demolished to make room for the new terminal's Pier G.

Pearson International Airport is a global transport facility, but it is foremost the Greater Toronto Area's airport. With the Greater Toronto Area increasing in global importance, the Pearson Airport of tomorrow will be a facility that supports growth and reflects the sophistication of the region. As the region continues to grow, so will its reliance on a world-class airport that is close to the business heart of Ontario. 🍁

In 1999, the extensive redevelopment program at Pearson Airport began to take shape (left).

"It is not a matter of 'if we build it, they will come,'" says GTAA President Louis A. Turpen. "We're building this airport because they are coming" (right).

Pearson International Airport is a global transport facility, but it is foremost the Greater Toronto Area's airport.

NTARIO POWER GENERATION (OPG) LIGHTS UP THE PROVINCE OF Ontario every day. As one of North America's major wholesale producers of electricity, OPG supplies municipal utilities, which, in turn, supply retail power to some 3 million homes and businesses. OPG also supplies electricity to

Hydro One, which distributes power to some 1 million customers, mainly in rural and remote parts of the province. About 100 large industrial and manufacturing customers also rely on the company.

OPG is a new company with a proud history. The firm was founded in April 1999 from the generation business of its predecessor, Ontario Hydro, which served Ontario's electricity needs for more than 90 years. In 2000, OPG's revenues were $5.9 billion with a net income of $605 million.

Building on its predecessor's legacy of service and reliability, OPG is committed to enhancing the quality of life in communities where it operates, producing competitively priced electricity products for its customers, and being an environmental leader.

COMMITTED TO THE COMMUNITY

Proud of its community involvement, OPG helped support more than 400 environmental, educational, and community organizations in 2000. Additionally, the company's employees raised more than $2.1 million in the same year for Ontario local community and charitable groups through the firm's annual Charity Campaign.

The company is also a powerful contributor to Ontario's economy. As a major employer of some 15,000 highly skilled individuals, OPG has a $1 billion-a-year payroll and spends

more than $1 billion annually in goods and services, primarily from Ontario-based suppliers. The company also returned more than $1.2 billion in taxes, dividends, and other payments to the province in 2000.

COMPETITIVE IN NORTH AMERICA

Jurisdictions around the world are in the process of opening up their energy markets to competition, and Ontario is no exception. OPG is well positioned to meet the challenges and opportunities of an emerging competitive marketplace.

A key strength is the company's diversified and flexible mix of nuclear, hydro-electric, and fossil-fuelled generating stations. This well-balanced generation mix enables OPG to reliably produce electricity that is cost competitive, safe, and clean.

OPG's nuclear performance index has steadily improved by more than 40 percent since the end of 1997—

moving the company closer to its ultimate goal of becoming a top-quartile nuclear operator worldwide.

To serve customers better in the new marketplace, OPG's Energy Markets Group recently opened a world-class energy-trading facility offering real-time electricity trading and dispatch capability, as well as the marketing of structured financial products and services.

OPG is also partnering with innovative companies to leverage and enhance the firm's expertise in areas such as information technology, research and development, and fuel-cell technology.

ENVIRONMENTAL LEADER

In an open market where consumers have choice, it is imperative to be identified as an environmental leader—especially given the growing importance the environment has with customers. OPG's approach to environmental issues is to be innovative and to lead change, not just respond to it.

OPG's high ratio of nuclear and hydro-electric facilities means that, from 1995 to 2000, more than 75 percent of the company's generation produced virtually no emissions contributing to acid gas, smog, or global warming. To reduce the environmental impact of its fossil-fuelled stations, OPG has invested more than $1.8 billion on pollution control technologies since 1984. These investments

Clockwise from top:
Ontario Power Generation (OPG) is one of North America's major wholesale producers of electricity.

The Darlington Generating Station in Durham region provides about 20 percent of Ontario's electricity needs.

The Sir Adam Beck Station at Niagara Falls has been in operation since 1922.

Wind-generated electricity can be used directly or fed into a transmission grid for use by all electricity consumers.

have enabled OPG's fossil stations to produce as much electricity as the company did in the early 1980s, but with almost 60 percent lower acid gas emissions.

OPG added to this commitment by announcing in 2000 that the company was investing $250 million to purchase four selective catalytic reduction units to further reduce nitrogen-oxide emissions at the firm's fossil-fuelled stations.

OPG's portfolio will be even cleaner with the planned return to service of the Pickering A nuclear station, which will be capable of annually displacing 13 million metric tons of greenhouse gases that otherwise would be generated by fossil-fuelled stations.

The company is also planning to quadruple its green energy portfolio sources from such sources as wind, the sun, and biomass to 500 megawatts by 2005.

In addition to these initiatives, OPG supports and participates in a number of environmental organizations, including the World Business Council on Sustainable Development; the E-7, consisting of eight of the world's leading electricity companies; and the Clean Energy Group,

composed of major electrical utilities in the northeast United States.

Since many of the company's facilities adjoin environmentally sensitive and significant areas, OPG also operates a number of innovative and important biodiversity and land/water management programs in the communities where the company operates. By 2006, for example, OPG will have planted some 1.6 million native trees and shrubs in southern Ontario to enhance biodiversity and to help offset carbon dioxide emissions, which contribute to global warming.

OPG was also one of the first utilities in North America to achieve ISO 14001 environmental accreditation at virtually all of its facilities in 1999. With the certification of its

small hydro operations in 2000, all OPG facilities are now accredited under this exacting international standard.

Internally, OPG exceeded its own energy savings targets for the seventh year in a row; through its energy efficiency program, the company has so far saved 2 million megawatt hours of power worth $85 million. For its success, OPG was awarded Canada's first National Energy Efficiency Award.

In short, Ontario Power Generation is making sustainable energy a key business priority, and is demonstrating that it is indeed possible to balance environmental leadership with social responsibility and solid financial performance. ♦

Clockwise from top left:
By 2006, OPG will have planted some 1.6 million native trees and shrubs in southern Ontario.

The Nanticoke fossil generating station is located on the north shore of Lake Erie.

OPG helped support more than 400 environmental, educational, and community organizations in 2000 as well as raising more than $2.1 million for Ontario local community and charitable groups.

The OPG Energy Markets facility includes a state of the art energy trading floor.

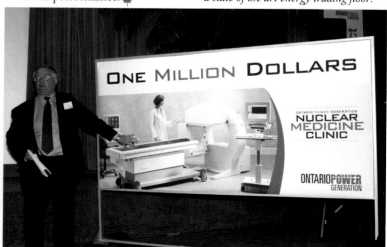

THE SCARBOROUGH HOSPITAL WAS CREATED ON SEPTEMBER 8, 1999, BY the voluntary amalgamation of the Scarborough General Hospital and the Salvation Army Scarborough Grace Hospital. Building on the traditions and strengths of its two founding partners, the merger was determined and designed by the two hospitals to bettter serve the community. The Scarborough Hospital provides a spectrum of care across its two full-service sites: the General Division and the Grace Division.

As one of Canada's largest community hospitals, The Scarborough Hospital has 650 beds and some 4,000 staff, 500 physicians, and 1,000 volunteers. Its purpose is to provide excellent patient care, foster research and education, and deliver a broad range of emergency, ambulatory, and in-patient care, along with services that reach out to the community.

The emergency department at The Scarborough Hospital is one of the busiest in the province with some 100,000 visits annually. The hospital sees some 6,000 babies born in its birthing centres each year, and provides a number of important services such as dialysis, magnetic resonance imaging (MRI), and a sexual assault centre. The hospital is also a referral centre for vascular surgery, orthopedics, pacemaker implants, and corneal implants.

The Scarborough Hospital provides a number of important services including magnetic resonance imaging (MRI).

LEADERSHIP IN RESEARCH AND EDUCATION

The Scarborough Hospital also fosters research and education that enhance health care delivery. Its educational partners, for example, include the University of Toronto Division of Family Medicine, Centennial College, and local high schools as well. More than 900 students—doctors, nurses, and allied health professionals from a broad range of disciplines—are trained at the hospital every year.

Ron Bodrug, President and CEO, explains: "Our founding hospitals have always been at the forefront of health care innovation—our list of firsts is long. It's a great tradition of innovation that we plan to continue." The history of Scarborough's founding hospitals includes several Canadian firsts: the first burn unit, the first psychiatric day treatment centre, the first sports medicine clinic, a groundbreaking corneal transplant program, and the first Ontario birthing centre. The Scarborough Hospital's physicians have been great innovators in new plastic surgery techniques, laparoscopic procedures, orthopedic surgery innovations, and emergency medicine. The hospital was the first in the province to introduce an innovative Web site feature called BabyLink, a virtual nursery that lets families from all over the world see their newborn relatives.

The Scarborough Hospital's leadership in patient care, education, and research could not continue without the generous support of both corporations and individuals. Byron Lawrence explains why his sister, Doris, so generously supported the hospital: "By leaving a gift in her will, Doris wanted to help the hospital continue to treat patients and their families in a caring and compassionate way."

The hospital is committed to building on its leadership role and moving forward as it fulfils its mission, achieves its vision, and lives its values.

CONNECTION WITH THE COMMUNITY

The Scarborough Hospital provides high-quality, compassionate care to a very broad catchment area that goes well beyond Scarborough to include Durham, York, and Toronto. It is a hospital that cares very much for this large and diverse community, and endeavours to meet the individual needs of the patients and families it serves.

State Farm, a corporate supporter of The Scarborough Hospital, describes the role the hospital plays in the community: "State Farm is pleased to assist The Scarborough Hospital as it serves so many in our community. This thriving health care operation is integral to Scarborough's continuing development."

The Scarborough Hospital values partnership with community groups who play an important role in determining needs and care. Members of the community sit on patient-care teams, and their input is actively sought.

The hospital reaches out to the community in a number of ways. It offers tours for new immigrants to familiarize them with the health care system, and runs special clinics for obtaining health cards. Among other culturally based services, the hospital participates in English as a second language (ESL) classes and organizes a Chinese In-Patient Support Group. To make certain that language is not a barrier, the hospital offers translation services in 48 languages and has multilingual directional signage and telephone systems.

Lieutenant-Colonel Irene Stickland, Executive Vice-President and Deputy CEO, adds, "We go above and beyond to meet the diverse needs of our community. Valuing, respecting, and caring for others is what makes this such a special hospital."

FORGING THE FUTURE

The future is bright for this dynamic urban hospital. The next major stage of The Scarborough Hospital's evolution will be a new critical care wing. Approved by the Ministry of Health and Long-Term Care, the new wing will include a much-expanded emergency service, a leading-edge diagnostic imaging department, a new coronary care unit, and an intensive care unit.

The Scarborough Hospital will continue to build on the values of its founding partners and the strength of its diversity. The hospital is committed to building on its leadership role and moving forward as it fulfills it mission, achieves its vision, and lives its values.

"We have been successful and will continue to be successful because of the tremendous support and commitment of our staff, physicians, and volunteers, as well as the people in our community," says Bodrug. "Through their support, we will continue to fulfill our commitment to caring for the community." 🍁

The Scarborough Hospital fosters research and education that enhance health care delivery.

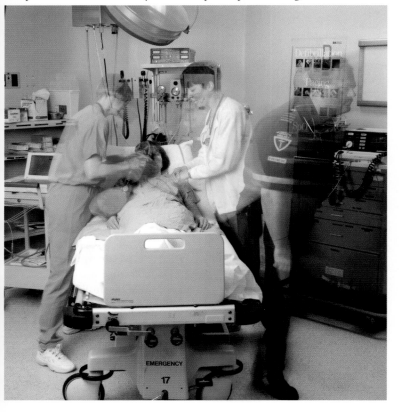

The purpose of the Scarborough Hospital is to provide excellent patient care, foster research and education, and deliver a broad range of emergency, ambulatory, and in-patient care.

EGINNING AS A SMALL PUBLISHER OF LOCAL NEWSPAPERS IN THE 1930s, Towery Publishing, Inc. today produces a wide range of community-oriented materials, including books (Urban Tapestry Series), business directories, magazines, and Internet publications. Building on its long heritage of excellence, the company has

become global in scope, with cities from San Diego to Sydney represented by Towery products. In all its endeavors, this Memphis-based company strives to be synonymous with service, utility, and quality.

A DIVERSITY OF COMMUNITY-BASED PRODUCTS

Over the years, Towery has become the largest producer of published materials for North American chambers of commerce. From membership directories that enhance business-to-business communication to visitor and relocation guides tailored to reflect the unique qualities of the communities they cover, the company's chamber-oriented materials offer comprehensive information on dozens of topics,

including housing, education, leisure activities, health care, and local government.

In 1990, Towery launched the Urban Tapestry Series, an award-winning collection of oversized, hardbound photojournals detailing the people, history, culture, environment, and commerce of various metropolitan areas. These coffee-table books highlight a community through three basic elements: an introductory essay by a noted local individual, an exquisite collection of four-color photographs, and profiles of the companies and organizations that animate the area's business life.

To date, nearly 90 Urban Tapestry Series editions have been published in cities around the world, from New York to Vancouver to Sydney. Authors

of the books' introductory essays include two former U.S. Presidents—Gerald Ford (Grand Rapids) and Jimmy Carter (Atlanta); boxing great Muhammad Ali (Louisville); Canadian journalist Peter C. Newman (Vancouver); two network newscasters—CBS anchor Dan Rather (Austin) and ABC anchor Hugh Downs (Phoenix); NBC sportscaster Bob Costas (St. Louis); record-breaking quarterback Steve Young (San Francisco); best-selling mystery author Robert B. Parker (Boston); American Movie Classics host Nick Clooney (Cincinnati); former Texas first lady Nellie Connally (Houston); and former New York City Mayor Ed Koch (New York).

To maintain hands-on quality in all of its periodicals and books, Towery has long used the latest production methods available. The company was the first production environment in the United States to combine desktop publishing with color separations and image scanning to produce finished film suitable for burning plates for four-color printing. Today, Towery relies on state-of-the-art digital prepress services to produce more than 8,000 pages each year, containing well over 30,000 high-quality color images.

AN INTERNET PIONEER

By combining its long-standing expertise in community-oriented published materials with advanced production capabilities, a global sales force, and extensive data management capabilities, Towery has emerged as a significant provider of Internet-based city information. In keeping with its overall focus on community resources, the company's Internet efforts represent a natural step in the evolution of the business.

The primary product lines within the Internet division are the introCity™ sites. Towery's introCity sites introduce newcomers, visitors, and long-time residents to every facet of a particular community, while simultaneously placing the local chamber

STEVE DAVIS

Towery Publishing President and CEO J. Robert Towery has expanded the business his parents started in the 1930s to include a growing array of traditional and electronic published materials, as well as Internet and multimedia services, that are marketed locally, nationally, and internationally.

of commerce at the forefront of the city's Internet activity. The sites include newcomer information, calendars, photos, citywide business listings with everything from nightlife to shopping to family fun, and on-line maps pinpointing the exact location of businesses, schools, attractions, and much more.

DECADES OF PUBLISHING EXPERTISE

In 1972, current President and CEO J. Robert Towery succeeded his parents in managing the printing and publishing business they had founded nearly four decades earlier. Soon thereafter, he expanded the scope of the company's published materials to include *Memphis* magazine and other successful regional and national publications. In 1985, after selling its locally focused assets, Towery began the trajectory on which it continues today, creating community-oriented materials that are often produced in conjunction with chambers of commerce and other business organizations.

Despite the decades of change, Towery himself follows a longstanding family philosophy of unmatched service and unflinching quality. That approach extends throughout the entire organization

to include more than 120 employees at the Memphis headquarters, and more than 40 sales, marketing, and editorial staff traveling to and working in a growing list of client cities. All of its products, and more information about the company, are featured on the Internet at www.towery.com.

In summing up his company's steady growth, Towery restates the essential formula that has driven the business since its first pages were published: "The creative energies of our staff drive us toward innovation and invention. Our people make the highest possible demands on themselves, so I know that our future is secure if the ingredients for success remain a focus on service and quality." 🍁

Towery Publishing was the first production environment in the United States to combine desktop publishing with color separations and image scanning to produce finished film suitable for burning plates for four-color printing. Today, the company's state-of-the-art network of Macintosh and Windows workstations allows it to produce more than 8,000 pages each year, containing more than 30,000 high-quality color images.

The Towery family's publishing roots can be traced to 1935, when R.W. Towery (far left) began producing a series of community histories in Tennessee, Mississippi, and Texas. Throughout the company's history, the founding family has consistently exhibited a commitment to clarity, precision, innovation, and vision.

Originally headquartered in London, **Allsport** has expanded to include offices in New York and Los Angeles. Its pictures have appeared in every major publication in the world, and the best of its portfolio has been displayed at elite photographic exhibitions at the Royal Photographic Society and the Olympic Museum in Lausanne.

Bruce Yuan-Yue Bi has traveled extensively in Canada, the United States, and Central and South America. He is a regular contributor to *Earth Geographic Monthly* in Taiwan and *Photo Pictorial Magazine* in Hong Kong.

Jan Butchofsky-Houser specializes in travel photography and has co-authored the third edition of a travel guidebook, *Hidden Mexico*. Her photos have appeared in dozens of magazines, newspapers, books, advertisements, and brochures, as well as on video and album covers. She has served as an editorial/research associate for the Berkeley, California-based Ulysses Press and currently manages Dave G. Houser Stock Photography. Her honours include two Bronze awards from the Society of American Travel Writers.

Originally from Chicago, **Brad Crooks** specializes in travel photography and owns B. W. Crooks Photographics.

Specializing in local and international area photography, **Ursula Easterbrook** has photographed various regions in North America. Her images have been displayed in solo slide and print shows and have won prizes both locally and nationally.

Specializing in travel, nature/wildlife, and rural photography, **Winston Fraser** has had images published in *National Geographic, Encyclopedia Britannica*, and the *New York Times*, as well as producing work for the Government of Canada and the Walt Disney Company. He has held many photo expositions for the benefit of various Christian charitable organizations.

Active in the Toronto photographic community for more than 20 years, **Dave Green** specializes in still photography. He has been involved in teaching and technical operations at the Ryerson Polytechnic Institute and has presented consistently in Toronto and Vancouver exhibitions since 1986.

David Griffith has worked internationally, producing portraiture and fashion and editorial photography. His images have appeared in *Equinox* and *Canadian Business*, and have also been sought by such businesses as Purolator Courier, Glaxo Pharmaceuticals, and IBM. He has been photographing Caribbean Carnivals for more than a decade and recently held a solo exhibit at the Smithsonian Institution.

A stock agency based in Toronto, **Hot Shots Stock Shots, Inc.** has contributed images to advertising and design agencies, publishers, major printing houses, large corporations, and manufacturers.

A contributing editor to *Vacations* and *Cruises & Tours* magazines, and co-author of the travel guidebook *Hidden Coast of California*, **Dave G. Houser** specializes in cruise/luxury travel, personality, health, and history photography. He has been a runner-up for the Lowell Thomas Travel Journalist of the Year Award and was named the 1984 Society of American Travel Writers' Photographer of the Year.

A specialist in natural history and stereophotography, **Bill Ivy** is the author/photographer of 24 books, including the award-winning *Close to Home*. His images have been published in books, magazines, calendars, and cards worldwide, and featured by more than 250 publishers, including the National Geographic Society, National Wildlife Federation, Sierra Club, Kodak, and Reader's Digest Association.

Brandon Klayman, a lifelong Torontonian, is a self-taught freelance photographer who combines his passion for music with his natural talent in photography. His work has appeared in numerous international publications and on album covers, and adorns the walls of many of the rock stars he has photographed. He uses his photographs to share his unique perspective of the world.

A Toronto-based research and photo assignment agency, **KLIX** specializes in the Canadian market and has performed assignments for editorial clients including *Time, People, Vanity Fair*, and many other Canadian magazines and book publishers. With a broad network of photographers ready to shoot assignments of any kind, KLIX's research department has worked on editorial projects for ABC-TV Biographies, McFarlane, Walter & Ross, McClelland & Stewart, and Key Publishers.

Originally from Cleveland, Ohio, **Betsy Molnar** specializes in editorial, commercial, and fine art black-and-white photography. She has contributed images to such publications as *Northern Ohio Live* and *Cleveland Magazine*, as well as to the Cleveland Clinic and numerous private collections.

Self-employed at Iconoclassic, **Judy Nisenholt** has had images published in magazines such as *Photo Life* and the *Sun*. Her photographs have focused on documenting the older, painted signage of Toronto using the Polaroid transfer medium.

Specializing in travel and fine art photography, **Richard Quataert** has traveled to more than 35 countries, photographing stills and movies for Kodak's multivision shows. His most recent shows include the Elizabeth Collection, the Austin Harvard Gallery, the Atrium Gallery, the Gallery at the Water Street Grill, and Classic Visions, and his *Photography in the Fine Arts* is on permanent display at the Metropolitan Museum of Art in New York.

© JONATHAN POSTAL / TOWERY PUBLISHING, INC.

Franco Rossi is a freelance photojournalist and specializes in travel, fashion, interior, and editorial photography. He has contributed images to such publications as *Capital*, *Elle*, and *Cosmopolitan*.

A four-time National Newspaper Award winner, **Boris Spremo** has had photographs included in many national and international publications such as books on Canada, *Sports Illustrated*, *Reader's Digest*, and *Time*. His photographic coverage includes more than 30 Royal Tours, the first Pan-American Games, the Kennedy funeral, the end of the Vietnam War, and worldwide royal weddings. He worked for the *Toronto Star* for more than 40 years.

A freelance editorial and commercial photographer, **Paul Till** employs various techniques, materials, equipment, and methodologies in his photography, and uses Toronto as the main subject or background of his work.

Originally from Besançon, France, **Emmanuel Vaucher** specializes in travel, people, sports, and candid shot photography. His images were published by Syracuse Language Systems—a language learning software producer—and appear in such publications as *Un Jour en France* and *Greater Syracuse: Center of an Empire*.

Owner of Mark Wilson Photography, **Mark Wilson** specializes in promotion and editorial photography and has had images included in such publications as the *Toronto Star* and the *Toronto Sun*. A user and supporter of digital technology, he has contributed images to publicity organizations such as the Big Brothers & Sisters of Canada.

Originally from Wisconsin, **Eric Wunrow** specializes in photography and graphic design. His images have sold worldwide in publishing and advertising media, often including text and graphics or illustrations of his own design.

Other contributing organizations include the Toronto Argonauts. Special thanks go to **KLIX** for its assistance to our photography editor Jonathan Postal. For further information about the photographers appearing in *Toronto: The World within a City*, please contact Towery Publishing.

◆ © MARK WILSON

LIBRARY OF CONGRESS CATALOGING-IN-PUBLICATION DATA

Toronto : the world within a city / introduction by Edwin Mirvish and David Mirvish ;
art direction by Robert Shatzer.
       p. cm. — (Urban tapestry series)
   Includes index.
   ISBN 1-881096-97-1 (alk. paper)
    1. Toronto (Ont.)—Civilization. 2. Toronto (Ont.)—Pictorial works. 3. Toronto
(Ont.)—Economic conditions. 4. Business enterprises—Ontario—Toronto.   I. Series.

F1059.5.T685 T67 2001
971.3'541—dc21

2001035151

Copyright © 2001 by Towery Publishing, Inc.

ALL RIGHTS RESERVED. NO PART OF THIS WORK MAY BE REPRODUCED OR COPIED IN ANY FORM OR
BY ANY MEANS, EXCEPT FOR BRIEF EXCERPTS IN CONJUNCTION WITH BOOK REVIEWS,
WITHOUT PRIOR WRITTEN PERMISSION OF THE PUBLISHER.

TOWERY PUBLISHING, INC., THE TOWERY BUILDING, 1835 UNION AVENUE, MEMPHIS, TN 38104
www.towery.com

PUBLISHER: J. Robert Towery EXECUTIVE PUBLISHER: Jenny McDowell MARKETING DIRECTOR: Carol Culpepper
PROJECT DIRECTORS: Pamela Alison Brady, Anthony Ingrassia, Brian Rhodes EXECUTIVE EDITOR: David B.
Dawson MANAGING EDITOR: Lynn Conlee SENIOR EDITORS: Carlisle Hacker, Brian L. Johnston PROJECT
EDITOR: Danna M. Greenfield EDITOR/ PROFILE MANAGER: Sabrina Schroeder EDITORS: Jay Adkins, Stephen
M. Deusner, Rebecca E. Farabough, Ginny Reeves PROFILE AND CAPTION WRITER: Lesley Byrne CREATIVE
DIRECTOR: Brian Groppe PHOTOGRAPHY EDITOR: Jonathan Postal PROFILE DESIGNERS: Rebekah Barnhardt,
Laurie Beck, Glen Marshall PRODUCTION MANAGER: Brenda Pattat PHOTOGRAPHY COORDINATOR: Robin
Lankford PRODUCTION ASSISTANTS: Robert Barnett, Robert Parrish DIGITAL COLOR SUPERVISOR: Darin Ipema
DIGITAL COLOR TECHNICIAN: Eric Friedl DIGITAL SCANNING TECHNICIANS: Brad Long, Mark Svetz PRINT
COORDINATOR: Beverly Timmons

[PRINTED IN HONG KONG]

INDEX OF PROFILES

© EMMANUEL FAGNEN

MW00569351